SO THIS IS HEAVEN
How Rescuing Old or Unwanted Dogs Provided a
Touch of Heaven on Earth

Monica Agnew-Kinnaman

CONTENTS

This book is dedicated to all the unfortunate creatures that are born and die without ever knowing the gift of love – the abused, the abandoned, the unwanted, and to all the special dogs that have shared my life.

FOREWORD

For many years it has been my privilege to take in old abused dogs that either I have found abandoned or that had already been rescued from a life of cruelty and misery but needed a loving home. This has been no self-sacrifice on my part. It has been as gratifying for me as for the victims who finally found their little piece of heaven in their "forever home" with me and my family. The dogs came from many sources and were just as likely to be a Great Dane or Irish Wolfhound as a Toy Poodle, or a mixed breed of unknown parentage. I loved them all.

Although of necessity I had a role in these stories, the main characters were the victims themselves. I only happened to be the one fortunate enough to be able to help them on their road to recovery, and without their strength and courage my efforts would have been useless.

For as long as I can remember I have always favored the underdog, the one struggling to live, and in his memoirs, many years ago, my father wrote of me: "Our youngest child was one who helped snails over the rough stones, tried to mend birds' broken wings … and brought home every mangy cat or stray dog she could find." This turned out to be a lifelong calling.

good care of him." I can hardly sit still I am in such a fever of anticipation.

"Would you like to see Jock?"

I am now almost beside myself with excitement as I say, "Oh, yes, yes. Please let me see him."

Mr. Robert reaches out to a bell on the wall. A manservant wearing a green baize apron appears and waits obsequiously in the doorway.

"Tom, bring Jock in here, please" his employer commands.

A few minutes later the man reappears with a tall, aristocratic-looking deerhound on a leash. The dog springs forward as soon as he sees Mr. Robert and lays his magnificent head in his master's lap. Robert strokes him absently while still addressing me.

"Well, what do you think, Missy? If you still want to take him, and you really think your parents wouldn't mind, you can have him." His eyes twinkle as he adds "And see if you can train him not to chase sheep."

I assure him that my parents won't mind one bit having a huge hound that takes off periodically to chase pregnant sheep. I don't know if he believes this fairy tale any more than I do myself, but I am determined that nothing will stop me from saving Jock.

"By the way", Mr. Robert is saying, "Have you had breakfast? How about a glass of milk and some cake?"

He is really very kind, I think to myself. In spite of the trophies on the wall I can't envisage him shooting Jock. Perhaps he would get the austere-looking butler to do it, or the manservant with the green baize apron.

After the milk and a slice of home-baked cake brought in by the cook, the hound is handed over to me by Mr. Robert, who wishes me the best of luck and says he is glad I came. He would like to know how Jock is doing from time to time, he says, as he gives Jock a pat on the head and tells him to be a good boy. Then the door is closed and I set off, wondering what my parents will say when I get home. But at the moment I am walking on air with excitement and happiness.

That was my first rescue.

My siblings and I grew up in Yorkshire, England before the Second World War, in the peace and tranquility of a beautiful English country village. By 1978, however, I had been in the United States of America for many years and at that point in time my own children were grown and, with only a husband and three dogs to contend with, my life was reasonably serene and uncomplicated. How I came to be in America is another story As children in England we had always had a multitude of animals of all shapes and sizes, from horses and donkeys to cats and dogs. Rabbits, guinea pigs, and even white mice were part of the menagerie, and each animal was chosen and loved until death did us part. I had never had cause to know much about abused and abandoned animals, but in 1978 my life was about to change significantly, and it all began with one little black dog.

ROSIE

I was driving towards the mountains on a bitterly cold winter's day in my Colorado home. The wind whipped through the streets, erratically blowing little puffs of icy snow that performed a ballet dance in front of my windshield before finally landing in a thick layer across the glass.

Peering out between the wipers' labored sweeps, I suddenly beheld a small, bedraggled bundle of fur darting in and out of traffic on this very busy thoroughfare, dodging cars in a frenzy of terror. I stepped on the brake sharply, skidding sideways in a maneuver that undoubtedly caused the other crawling drivers to turn the white, freezing air blue with expletives.

By the time I had managed to steer my pickup perilously to the curb, the dog was standing, bewildered and shaking, in the comparative safety of a side street. I heaved myself out of my truck, battling several layers of heavy underwear and a huge, Arctic-type coat, all of which seemed to be doing their best to pin me to the driver's seat.

I approached the dog slowly on foot, and only by the grace of an understanding God managed to stay upright as I slipped and slid towards it on the ice. My fear was that in its confused state it would make a mad dash back into the stream of traffic, and I remember addressing it with soothing, nonsensical phrases, which were all I could muster in this time of crisis.

"Good doggy. How are you doing today?" (A silly question under the circumstances.) "What awful weather we are having. Are you very cold?"

Something worked. Rather to my surprise it allowed itself to be scooped up into my arms, nestling its cold, wet nose against my neck.

There was a small grocery store around the corner and I carried the shivering little creature inside, hoping that someone would come forward to claim it. Instead, the manager approached, asking if he could be of any assistance.

"Yes," I replied, grateful for any kind of help. "Have you seen this dog before? I thought it might belong to one of your customers."

Smiling cheerfully, he told me that the dog had been hanging around his store for three days, darting inside whenever a customer entered and picking up any scraps of discarded food it could find on the floor. He assured me that he and his employees had chased it out time after time, shouting at it and even using a broom to frighten it out on to the street, but it always came back.

"I'm surprised," he concluded, still smiling, "that it's alive. I thought it would have been run over by now."

His callousness appalled me and by this time my frustration was so great I could hardly contain my anger. I wanted to yell at him, "Why didn't you just pick up the phone and call the Humane Society?" But I knew it would be a losing battle so, without another word, I stalked out of the store carrying my little bundle.

Once outside I stood on the sidewalk, not knowing what I was going to do next. I already had three dogs at home, besides which I was due to attend a university in North Dakota for several weeks, starting in less than a month. My husband would care for our own dogs while I was gone, but I was sure he would be less than thrilled to have another member of the four-legged variety dumped on him. By now I had discovered that my new charge was female, appeared to be two or three years old and was painfully thin. She also had a suspiciously large belly for such a small dog. That, I thought, is all I need.

I decided there was nothing I could do but carry her to my vehicle that stood at the side of the road in a welter of mud and ice. I felt confident that a solution would present itself before I got home. Unfortunately, it didn't.

"I don't know who you are." I said to the little figure, which was now sitting, demurely by my side, "but you have to have a name. Just temporarily." I assured her. So I named her forthwith, and she became "Rosie, little girl of the streets." The name stuck.

My husband was not yet home from work when I sneaked into the house with Rosie under one arm. Expertly bypassing my three dogs on the way, the first thing I did was to run a warm bath with plenty of doggy shampoo, and by the time I had cleaned off all the dirt and smells of a neglected little body, treated her infected runny eyes and combed out her curly black hair, she was quite beautiful.

I had never had such a little dog before. Even in childhood my dogs had mostly been of the massive variety, almost able to knock you over by just looking at you, so Rosie was a miniature canine novelty for me.

After admiring my handiwork, I started to clean the tub and gather up all the paraphernalia which goes along with bathing dogs — dripping towels, empty shampoo bottle, messy floor and hair-clogged drain. I had just finished when I heard my husband's key in the door. I ran downstairs to cut him off at the pass.

"Honey," I said ingratiatingly, "I have a surprise."

"Let me guess, he shot back jokingly, "You've brought a horse home and you're keeping it in our bedroom." He knew me too well.

"You're close," I said, "but it's not a horse. It's a dog. Just a very, very little dog."

"Oh, God," he groaned, "What did I do to deserve this!"

I was not due in North Dakota until the latter part of January, so this gave me almost a month to figure out what to do with Rosie. In the following days there were no replies to ads in the newspapers and on notice boards, and the local Humane Society had no record of a lost dog fitting her description. By the end of ten days I was resigned to the fact that Rosie was mine, for better or worse. On Christmas Day she opened her present along with the rest of us, including Paddy (our 170 lb Irish Wolfhound), Jenny (a Shetland Sheepdog/Australian Shepherd mix), and Becky (an Australian Cattle Dog).

Paddy had been with us almost since birth, the product of an aristocratic and distinguished family of wolfhounds, carefully nurtured from the moment they saw the light of day. Not so Jenny. My daughter and I had found her many years before, huddled pitifully under a seething mass of assorted puppy bodies in a mall, at a pet store where we had gone to buy food for Roger, my son's fat, cuddly guinea pig. Roger, incidentally, was allowed to gallop around the lawn each day under minimal supervision, and would come when he was called. I always felt this was quite an achievement for a guinea pig, even though it happened to be an achievement reinforced with treats!

"Mum," my daughter had called, ("Mum" being the English equivalent of "Mom"), do come and look at this puppy. "He can't get comfortable, and they are all lying on him."

I walked over to the small cage where about eight puppies were competing noisily and persistently for space, and peered at the bottom of the heap. Sure enough, a small, golden-brown body was vainly struggling to free itself from the squirming mass, emitting plaintive cries of fear and pain.

At that time Frosty, our beloved old Samoyed, had developed cancer and was about to journey to the Happy Hunting Grounds. There was no more our doggy doctor could do for him. Frosty had always loved small things, including puppies, so I had no qualms regarding what I was about to say.

"How would you like to take him home?" I asked Susie.

"Oh, can we?" she breathed excitedly. "Please, Mum."

So Jenny, who turned out to be a she, not a he, became the newest member of the family. After we took her home we discovered that she was a very sick little pup and had to be under the care of our veterinarian for several weeks. In addition, she had a badly broken tail, which was not immediately noticeable under her thick coat of puppy fur.

Jenny became one of our most beloved dogs. A true sheepdog, she was always obedient, anxious to please, and completely devoted to the whole family. If we had to leave the house for any length of time, when we got home it was to find that she had gathered pieces of everybody's clothing, sometimes from the dirty clothes hamper, into a neat little pile and was lying on top of them. She lived a long and happy life, finally succumbing to a massive stroke at the age of fifteen years and eight months.

The third member of our canine family that winter was Becky, an Australian cattle dog. Becky came to us by way of a friend who became terminally ill and was unable to care for her. She was a sweet, loving dog with a penchant for walking about on top of our dining room table when no one was looking.

Rosie flourished with all the TLC she was receiving, and as her thin little body filled out, her tummy expanded accordingly, mute evidence of an unfortunate doggy union somewhere on the streets. Our resident dogs accepted her cheerfully and she easily accommodated to our way of life, but I was still wondering how to deal with a tricky situation. I was soon to leave for North Dakota and my husband's protests were becoming louder and more insistent. With a demanding job, Jim felt that four dogs were too much, especially as one was "expecting."

Just as I was beginning to despair, a phone call saved the day. It was from an acquaintance who had been recommended to us by a close friend. She was looking for a small dog to be a companion to her own beloved Shih Tzu puppy. She traveled occasionally and felt he needed "someone to talk to" in addition to the housekeeper while she was away. She had heard of Rosie through mutual friends but was unaware of her pregnancy. I explained the situation, and amidst cries of delight — actually from both of us — she happily agreed to take a complete family of mother and yet-to-be-born pups. I knew this would be a doggy home made in heaven, and though I was sad to part with her, I handed Rosie over with complete confidence.

I only saw my "little girl of the streets" once more. It was several months later, and long after I returned from North Dakota. She recognized me immediately and ran up to me, abbreviated tail wagging furiously, but within minutes she had disappeared out into the garden through a doggy door in search of her Shih Tzu friend.

I was overjoyed to hear that the three puppies had all been relocated to good homes, but most of all I was thankful to hear that Rosie had been spayed!

My next encounter with a dispossessed canine found me with the antithesis of Rosie, and which appeared in the shape of an enormous Irish Wolfhound — reputed to be the tallest breed of dog on the planet. I first encountered him on the west side of town, and whether lost or abandoned I never knew.

When I first saw him he was standing alone, a solitary figure on a vast expanse of mesa. There were no houses or buildings of any kind in sight, and it was very obvious that a dog alone had no business there. He appeared to be young, two or three years old, and from the length of his wheaten-colored body I judged him to be well over six feet tall when standing on his hind legs. This estimate was reached by mentally comparing him with Paddy, my own Irish Wolfhound who had come to us as a monstrously huge eight-week-old puppy. Now, when standing upright on his back legs, Paddy dwarfed my five foot eleven inch husband. This present, fearsome-looking creature, besides having an unbelievably elongated body, was extremely thin and looked as though he had spent many days and nights in the open.

I climbed out of my truck to take a closer look. I was uncomfortably aware of the fact that any dog this size, especially when agitated, could pose a significant threat to life and limb and this great hound was standing stock still, inspecting me with an unwavering stare and a frightening resemblance to the Hound of the Baskervilles, a horror film I saw as a child. To make matters worse, an article I had read many years ago flashed persistently through my mind.

In essence, it warned that any dog confronting you with tail elevated and slightly crouched body, while staring you fixedly in the eye, is preparing to attack. This, I now know, is not strictly true because Max, my kindly Old English Sheepdog, who has a grotesque addiction to food, frequently adopts this attitude. Of course Max has no tail to elevate, but at the mere whiff of food this normally quiet, well-behaved senior citizen is transformed into a salivating monster. Eyes riveted on the face of anyone he happens to find eating, he, too, assumes a crouched position, preparing to spring should a crumb fall. But this particular day was pre-Max, and I could not help but feel a little nervous when confronted by this canine giant.

On the face of things, I decided, the best line of defense was to do nothing at all. So, following the hound's example, I stood motionless as we summed each other up. By this time we were about twenty yards apart and as I surreptitiously glanced towards the open truck door, my only escape route a short distance away, I wondered what his next move was going to be. Undoubtedly he was having the same thoughts about me. I started to talk to him, gently and quietly, in tones that I hoped he would recognize as a friendly overture. After a few minutes of verbal drivel on my part he started towards me, head held low and eyes fixed on mine.

The lowered head I found rather alarming, but I couldn't detect any outward signs of aggression — no lips drawn back to reveal drooling fangs, no raised hackles, no guttural sounds cruising towards me from his huge, hairy throat. And remembering the article's warning, "together with lowered head, a raised tail is a red flag," I noted with relief that the tail was firmly planted between his hind legs. Discreetly extending my arm in case he decided he would like to take a sniff at my hand, I waited as he approached, slowly and cautiously. After a few seconds the tail emerged from between his hind legs and started to swing slowly from side to side. He laid his great head on my arm, and I knew I had him.

Backing away, uttering words of comfort and occasionally humming snatches of song like an old-time cowboy soothing his herd of cattle, I reached my pickup with the hound closely following. The one dog I had with me was on the front seat, anchored with a home-made seat belt, so I opened the tailgate and with a sigh of relief watched this huge animal jump into the back of the truck and settle himself comfortably on the floor.

My long-suffering husband looked out of the kitchen window just in time to see me walking up the garden path, and I could imagine his horror and desperation when he realized what was accompanying me. But, as usual, he adapted to the situation, especially as I pleaded, "Just for a few days, honey. We'll find his family."

Our dogs, as they always did, accepted a strange body into their midst graciously. But to be on the safe side their natural curiosity was limited to a few daily sniffs through a wire fence before being allowed a cautious introduction, nose to nose. Eventually the new wolfhound was allowed to inspect each room in the house. He never once lifted a giant leg to mark his new territory, which in view of his size was a blessing. He seemed very content.

As with Rosie, there were no replies to my ads and notices pleading for his special person to come forward and claim him, so he was blessed with a good old Irish name, Timothy O'Brien, and established himself comfortably into our over-crowded household.

At this point I feel it is only fair to say that, in the years since we had been married, Jim had undergone a dramatic change. He grew up on a cattle ranch where all animals, dogs and cats included, were lumped together as "critters." Understandably, those falling under the category of "useful critters" were horses, barnyard cats and working cattle dogs, all of which earned the right to eat well and sleep in a warm barn, or outside in the open if they chose to do so. "Pets," on the other hand, were viewed rather disdainfully as parasites, which lounged, about the house, becoming fat and lazy at the expense of indulgent masters. "No animals in the house" was his rule before we were married. But with the advent of Frosty, the Samoyed he chose himself after five years of marriage, his attitude started to change, bolstered by a little calculated encouragement from me.

I had been longing for a dog as soon as we moved from an apartment into our own house, which had a spacious fenced yard and a large lawn. One of his friends had two Samoyeds, and Jim was impressed by their huge white coats that enabled them to live comfortably outside in the coldest weather. Frosty, one year old at the time, was advertised in the local newspaper, and Jim decided it was the perfect dog for us.

The change that I had wanted so badly came about over time, in small increments. At first, Frosty was relegated to the garden and the outside porch, then to the kitchen, and finally allowed into the living room for short visits. After a couple of months he had the run of the house, while Jim ended up embracing the lost and battered dog-rescue-syndrome almost as enthusiastically as I had myself.

Timothy O'Brien lived with us for a few months and could have spent the rest of his life with us, but unfortunately not every rescue has a fairy tale ending. As he settled in I noticed him becoming more and more territorial with each passing day. He was passive and affectionate with all humans, but I had to constantly watch him with my gentle Paddy, and even with Jenny and Becky.

The two wolfhounds were roughly the same size, and although Paddy was heavier, Tim was younger, taller, and more muscular. As he put on weight, thanks to a healthy diet and enormous appetite, I realized he was becoming a real danger to Paddy, often with bared teeth and threatening stance as he tried to establish dominance.

Paddy was the proverbial "lover not fighter," which was made very clear to me when he was about three years old. At that time I was taking my usual daily walk in the country with the dogs when a cat popped up out of the underbrush like a Jack-in-the Box, literally under Paddy's nose. It had obviously been hunting, and now became the hunted. A sudden rush of adrenaline was too much for the hound's self-control and ignoring my shrieked commands, which rose dramatically in volume and intensity each second, a blur of huge gray dog and small calico cat rapidly vanished out of sight into a wooded area. Panting heavily, I sped after them in the direction of the trees, fully expecting to find a lifeless cat in Paddy's huge jaws. Instead, to my astonishment, I found it backed up against a wooden shed, hissing spitefully as Paddy lovingly tried to lick its face. Clearly, Paddy was a pushover. He wouldn't stand a chance in a knockdown, drag-out dogfight.

With Tim the deciding factor came one fall day, roughly three months after he was adopted into our family. We were walking in a nearby park, just he and I. He had obviously had little training in proper leash behavior, and I always felt I could cope with him best alone. This way, with no other dogs to distract either one of us, I could start teaching him not to pull, to walk on the left side, to heel when told, and all the other little niceties that made life so much more enjoyable for the dog-walker.

All was well until a Cocker Spaniel appeared, running loose with no "special person" in sight. I could feel Tim stiffen and saw the hackles raised on his back. In spite of my cordial warning shouts (like "Get out of here, you little moron"), the stranger continued to advance, waggling his bottom and peeing deferentially as he started towards Tim. The latter gave a fearsome roar and plunged forward to the end of his leash. The other dog fled, short legs pounding the ground and long spaniel ears streaming out behind him.

Unfortunately, Tim set off in hot pursuit and I was dragged behind him, my feet scarcely touching the ground. To any onlooker, had there been one hovering in the bushes, I must have closely resembled the Flying Nun about to take off. There was no way I could keep up with this powerful juggernaut, and I was soon yanked off my feet and on to my stomach. The weight of my body being hauled along the ground behind him, still grimly hanging on to the leash, slowed Tim down and the smaller dog disappeared out of sight over the horizon. It was very clear that Timothy O'Brien had a murderous intent, and I knew I had no choice.

That same day I called an Irish Wolfhound rescue group and explained the situation. They listened patiently, asked a few questions, and then told me they would be glad to find a good home where Tim would be an only child. In fact they said they already had the perfect solution. True to their word, within a week a big, husky young man who looked as if he could throw a steer with ease had driven a thousand miles from one of the south-western states to pick Tim up.

"He may be a fighter," I told him tentatively. I knew it could be the under-statement of the year, but I felt this young Texan was equal to the challenge.

"No problem," he answered cheerfully. "We'll work on that." They bonded immediately, and Timothy O'Brien disappeared on the front seat of an enormous pickup truck with nary a backward glance.

I kept in touch with Tim's "special person" for several months and learned they were inseparable. Things couldn't have turned out better. I had been truly sorry to see Tim go, but weighing the pros and cons, it was a tremendous relief!

Following the Tim saga there had been several brief encounters with straying canines where I had been able to return them to their respective homes before they were squashed under the wheels of oncoming traffic.

There was the golden retriever puppy coursing down the street after his "person" had carelessly left the garden gate open; there were the two Rottweilers that had followed an unsuspecting delivery man out of the yard, and which I spotted competing with eighteen wheelers as they raced down the interstate, one of them already bleeding. I honked my horn several times and when I slowed down behind them they moved over to the side of the road. As I stopped my vehicle I found they were already waiting for me. They were very friendly and I found them both quite ready to take orders. The injured male was able to crawl onto the floor of the passenger side, while the female jumped into the back of my truck as soon as I opened the tailgate. They had only one out-of-date tag between them, but their family was so overjoyed to have them home that it made the effort of tracing them worthwhile. When they offered to reward me Jim had a wonderful suggestion — donate food to an animal rescue group. This they were delighted to do, and their generous contribution was gratefully received.

Finally, there was the little gray mutt, which had been missing for several days and was welcomed back into the bosom of his family with tears and squeals of joy.

But that was not all. There was the starving cat in a drainage ditch, which ended up being deposited with a cat rescue group. I would have gladly kept him, but with so many dogs I feared for his safety. There was the pigeon, discovered lying on the sidewalk after ingesting poison that had been left illegally, and specifically for pigeons inhabiting the neighborhood, and a hawk that had inadvertently flown into telephone wires and suffered a broken wing. Both of these were resuscitated, and rehabilitated by a veterinarian who was certified to treat wildlife.

There was even a skunk that had been hit by a car and left to die on the road. He looked up at me with little bright questioning eyes as I draped an old blanket around him - one that I kept in the back of my vehicle for emergencies such as this. Having cautiously covered both head and rear end, I laid him in the back of my truck. He didn't attempt to fight or spray me, and that alone was an indication that he was badly hurt.

I drove to the nearest vet's office and went inside, leaving the inert figure on the floor of my pickup.

"I have an injured wild animal in my truck" I said. "It's been hit by a car. Could your doctor take a look at him?"

"Oh, of course," the girl behind the desk replied brightly. "We often have people bring little wild things in that have been injured. Is it a squirrel?"

"No," I ventured, avoiding her gaze. "Actually, it's a skunk." She let out a little shriek of horror, and all her former complacency disappeared, together with her smile.

"A skunk" she mouthed in disbelief. Then "A SKUNK!" she repeated in icy terms, with great emphasis on the last word. "We don't treat SKUNKS."

"What should I do then?" I asked. "He's hurt."

"Take it to the Wildlife people," she said, regaining her composure with an effort. "And good luck."

An officer at the Division of Wildlife carried the skunk gently into the holding area and promised faithfully (under a certain amount of pressure from me) that it would not be destroyed if it could be successfully treated and released into the wild. I left with my fingers and toes crossed.

Lastly, there was a mouse of the field variety that I stopped to peer at on the road, but it was beyond help. It really was quite dead.

By this time I had begun to entertain the horrible suspicion that I was surrounded by some kind of magnetic field that diabolically sucked needy creatures into its orbit specifically for me to care for. After much thought and deliberation I promised myself that if I saw one more lost, abandoned, or malfunctioning creature I would take instant flight in the opposite direction. But, things don't always work out the way you want them to.

SHEBA

It was another of those bitterly cold winter days when the temperature hovered around ten degrees Fahrenheit. It had snowed for several days, but by the time I decided that my dogs and I were suffering from a mild case of cabin fever the snow had already stopped falling.

I left the house accompanied by Paddy, Jenny, and Brandy, the latter a beige, strikingly beautiful Russian Wolfhound/Collie cross that we had recently adopted from the pound. Jim, who had become almost as fanatical as I to the cause of these pitiful creatures, had heard from a friend that a badly beaten dog had been at the shelter for over a week. Although unusually meek and gentle, she had been labeled "unadoptable" because of her extreme fear of all people. Her time was up and a death sentence had been pronounced for the following day. We decided to try and beat the deadline, and asked to see her before the sentence was carried out.

We were shown into a wire enclosure where she was lying alone on the cement floor. The hopeless, stricken look in her eyes, the cringing posture and malnourished body decided us immediately. We took her home that day and with time, patience, and lots of love, this beautiful creature blossomed into another of our most beloved companions. At first she belly-crawled on the ground whenever anyone came near, even members of the family. She bolted upstairs, taking refuge under a bed if a stranger should appear, and it was more than a year before she gained enough self-confidence to meet neighbors and friends without fear. Gradually, she realized that she was safe from harm or punishment, and when the other dogs raced to greet us as we returned from some mission, it was gratifying to see that Brandy was often in the lead. One of her greatest joys was to run, fulfilling her wolfhound heritage, and on quiet country roads, far from traffic, she was allowed to expend her vast energy trying to beat my pickup truck. She ate well so her thin body soon filled out, revealing an impressively aristocratic looking figure. She craved affection and her greatest joy was to be with us wherever we went, and to snuggle up beside us when night came.

On this particular December day the dogs were all eager for a romp in the snow, their thick coats protecting them from the icy weather. I had driven some three miles out of town, and then followed a track on foot. The track led over a large area of open ground with only a few leafless bushes to be seen. Walking briskly, I crunched over the snow and ice as the dogs scattered, searching diligently for any interesting smells. Sometimes a ball of snow would collect on their pads and they stopped to gnaw it loose, or occasionally run back to me so that I could scrape it off. Otherwise the cold ground did not seem to bother them.

After about twenty minutes I'd had enough, and I turned back towards the truck. It was late afternoon and the skies were already darkening. The temperature had dropped abruptly and ominously, typical of mountain country, and lights from the distant town had begun to twinkle on the skyline. The mountains, stunningly beautiful in the daytime, now looked dark and foreboding. As I hurried towards my vehicle, which was parked about half a mile away, I could feel the intense cold seeping through my thick winter clothing, urging me into a trot.

What caused me to stop and look back has remained one of those mysteries that sometimes lurk in the back of one's mind, and for which there is no explanation. I can only think my magnetic field was working overtime because something compelled me to stop and turn around. Outlined against a small hillock, behind and to the left of me, a large black head rose slowly out of the gloom. A body was not visible, so whatever it was had to be in a sitting or lying position. After a few moments of peering through the gathering dusk, I was able to recognize the head and neck of a black Great Dane.

To go home to a warm house, leaving this dog alone in such a frigid environment, seemed to be out of the question, but I was afraid my own boisterous canine family would cause it to take fright and disappear into the darkness. So, with this in mind, I hurried them back to my pickup as fast as I could, and once they were safely installed in the back I made my way down the track again. Under a small, naked bush, far off the beaten path, I saw a Great Dane crouched, shivering uncontrollably in its sparse coat. It looked as if it had made a pathetic attempt to build a little nest for itself, scratching mud and dead leaves into a small pile under the leafless bush. Squatting down on the ground, I tried to coax it towards me but it was almost paralyzed with fear. Each time I moved forward it backed away, crouching close to the ground, and I soon realized that I was going to have to try another tack. I made a beeline for my truck.

Fortunately, only two or three vehicles were on the road, so I covered the three miles to my home in record time. Once there I flung open the tailgate and herded my surprised trio into the house at a dead run. I was working against time as once full darkness set in my chances of finding the dog again were slim. Jim was still at work but Susie, my sixteen-year-old daughter, was somewhere in the confines of the house, busily immersed in homework. Yelling for her to come on the double, I started rummaging in the refrigerator. I found a package of hamburger meat and threw it into a frying pan. As soon as it was hot enough to exude an irresistibly delicious fragrance I grabbed the pan and, with Susie in tow, made another mad dash for the pickup.

We reached the track as all light was fading and the frigid air hit us with full force, numbing our cheeks and lips. Luckily for us, the snow provided us with enough reflected light to guide us and we were able to locate the same leafless bush. After a few moments we saw the dog's black head and long neck rising up from behind the hillock as the aroma of half-cooked hamburger meat floated towards it on the night air. Minutes passed as we waited, then hunger triumphed over fear. With shoulders hunched down and tail clamped under its body, it slowly crept towards us. Susie held out the meat as I waited in the background, watching protectively. The dog started to eat, gently taking the food out of Susie's hand and allowing her to slip her fingers under its worn collar.

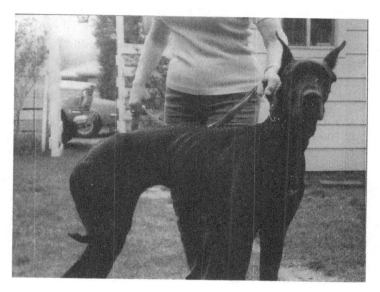

I was proud of the way my daughter unflinchingly led the dog to the back of the pickup and climbed in, the Great Dane following her as she held on to the collar. The two of them sat on the floor of the truck together, the dog huddling up against her as she stroked its face and put her arm around the starved body. When we arrived home Susie led the Dane, a female, up to her bedroom and covered her with a blanket to thaw out her half-frozen skin.

As soon as I had disposed of the truck into the garage and the frying pan into the sink, I went to inspect our latest guest. She was lying on the bed, and as I pulled back the blanket that covered her I could count every rib. I think her eyes were the saddest I had ever seen, as though haunted by horrible experiences known only to her. There were no tags on her frayed collar so we had no way of identifying her. Needless to say, she stayed with us until her poor emaciated body recovered from weeks or months of starvation. According to the veterinarian who examined her, she was about five years old and in good basic health. As she recovered she turned out to be sweet and loving, especially devoted to Susie whom she obviously regarded as her savior.

One could only wonder what this dog's life had been. Had she escaped from a bad home? Had she been thrown out to fend for herself? Had she been a cherished companion that had somehow become separated from her own family? Or had she been stolen, and abandoned when the perpetrators no longer wanted to bother with her? These were unanswered questions, which plagued me with every homeless dog we found.

As with Tim, there was no way we could add her permanently to our present menagerie of animals, although for different reasons. Sheba, as she was eventually named, was friendly and mixed well with the other dogs, but now we had more animals than we had planned on, and even one more was going to be a burden, both physically and financially.

There was a Great Dane rescue group in the phone book, and I contacted them after a few weeks of concentrated nurturing to which Sheba responded gratefully. One day I received a call telling me that there was a couple who had just lost their beloved Dane and were eager to give our "rescue" a permanent, loving home. And that is what it turned out to be. She lived with them for the rest of her life, and from the photos they sent me from time to time I knew that Sheba had found happiness in her own little heaven on earth.

JUNEAU

Juneau was a little Arctic wolf pup and how I was fortunate enough to become her caregiver, companion, and lifelong friend is another story altogether. At this time it is sufficient to say that I was the one privileged to receive and raise this enchanting little creature.

NOTE: The author does not in any way encourage or condone transplanting wild animals of any kind into the home as "pets" or companions. Wolves and wolf hybrids are not dogs and can be a danger to both small and large animals, and even to the person who is trying to nurture them. The wolf is always a wolf at heart, and high percentage wolf-hybrids possess the same wild instincts as the wolf itself. This trait, together with the lack of fear of humans inherited from the dog parent, can be a dangerous combination at the best of times. But this is the story of only one little wolf that, at that particular point in time, needed someone to care for her, and that someone happened to be me.

Juneau was born in the mountains and when she came into my life, a very small wolf pup inducted into a large and sometimes hostile world, she was only about five weeks old. A few generations before her birth an adventurous husky had invaded the wolf gene pool, and although it was estimated that she was about 94% pure wolf, Juneau's slight but significant dog heritage precluded any thought of abandoning her to the wild. Without any parents to guide her she would soon have perished. But she needed a home, and while I was eager to love and care for her I had some serious misgivings. Was I too old to take on such a responsibility? Could I give her the kind of home she deserved? What would happen to her if she outlived me? And, most importantly, what wolf traits were lurking in the sweet, innocent-looking little body? As I held the diminutive ball of warm, black fur against me, huddled under my chin, I knew that all my doubts and fears were of no consequence — I would take her anyway. So I wrapped her in a blanket, bade farewell to those who cared as deeply as I about her future, and climbed into my pickup with my precious little bundle.

Our first night was spent in a mountain cabin, and although she was capable of chewing I gave her a bottle of prepared formula to help cement our relationship, holding her in my lap upside down as she sucked noisily on the rubber teat. She had formidably sharp little baby teeth, and after the bottle she took a small amount of chopped meat with gusto. Her black fur was thick and soft, with a narrow white streak running down her chest in contrast to her coal-black body. Her fat little tummy caused her to waddle slightly while her long, thickly furred tail helped her to maintain her balance. After she had eaten I lifted her onto the rough-hewn bed in the corner. She crept under the blanket and we fell asleep together quite harmoniously. But in the morning she was gone. I searched under the blankets, but there was no sign of her. I knew there was no way she could have escaped outside, and finally located her in the darkest corner under the bed.

I squirmed my way towards her on my stomach and was astonished to hear a hissing sound, like an angry snake, followed by a horrible skunk-like odor that caused me to gag and back off quickly. A few weeks later, when talking to one bearded old-timer who could easily have passed for a mountain man from the eighteen hundreds, I mentioned this curious phenomenon. He nodded sagely.

"That's what the young'uns do when their mamas ain't there to protect 'em," he announced, with great authority. "Them babies make like they're snakes or skunks to scare off anything lookin' to eat 'em."

True or not, from my own experience this seemed to make sense, and anyway, I found the thought of baby wolves "making like snakes and skunks" quite intriguing!

As it happened, that was the one and only time Juneau subjected me, or anyone else, to that kind of treatment, and by the time we reached home she seemed to be comfortable with her new situation. I continued to give her a bottle for as long as she wanted it, and to further enhance the bonding process I "wore" her in a little sling around my neck, breathing into her nostrils as she breathed into mine. She traveled everywhere with me in this fashion until she grew too heavy for comfort.

I hand-fed her, and when she snatched morsels of meat, her sharp little teeth grinding into my hand until they drew blood, I wrapped the meat around a teaspoon. Without hurting her, the hard metal taught her to take food gently and with restraint — a habit that remained with her for the rest of her life.

She became a joy to the whole family, except for one little problem. Teaching Juneau to potty in the garden instead of in her favorite spot under the dining room table was a chore that stretched everyone's patience to the limit. Happily, at three months old she finally understood what was expected of her and never made the same mistake again. At six months she could jump like a deer and all the fences were raised to a height of ten feet. But we needn't have worried because Juneau had no intention of leaving home.

There were times when she had to be chastised, but she was never physically punished. A stern word of reproof was all it took for the ears to flatten, the head to lower in mock shame, and the body to roll over, belly up, in the classical pose of submission. As soon as she had made her point and knew she was forgiven she leaped to her feet, carrying on about her business as though nothing had happened. And, because she was always treated with gentleness and respect, she herself learned to be gentle and loving in return.

There had always been a multitude of cherished "pets" in my life since early childhood. In England there were horses and dogs, cats and rabbits, and even white mice which occasionally escaped to mate with the wild mice, returning to their cages to give birth to an odd collection of white and gray offspring. My father was a "people doctor," an MD who patiently treated a variety of injured wild creatures that my brother and I, from time to time, found in the woods and fields and brought home to be healed and then set free. I loved them all, but Juneau and I bonded closer than any other animal and I had ever done before.

As she matured her incredible super-intelligence began to reveal itself. Spontaneously, she learned to point with outstretched paw at the refrigerator, a carton of milk on the counter, or anything else she happened to fancy. To our dismay, she learned to open latched gates and turn knobs, which meant doubling security on all entrances and exits. She skillfully used paws and teeth to pull the blankets off me when she thought I should be up, which was usually at dawn, and when I resisted she would rush me, with bared teeth and ferocious growls.

But the prancing gait and wagging tail reassured me that it was all part of a game.

I remember waking from a deep sleep one night to find her straddling me, two feet on either side of my body, almost pinning me to the bed in her efforts to arouse me. Her face was close against mine as she clawed frantically at the top of my head, her powerful paws deliberately skirting my upturned face. As I slowly came to my senses I smelled smoke. A small fire, caused by faulty wiring, had started in my bedroom and the carpet was already starting to burn. Sam, my six-year-old wolfhound, still snoozed peacefully by the bedside, totally oblivious of the danger, while our old sheepdog, Jenny, wandered nervously around the room. It was Juneau who knew instinctively that she must wake me.

Once the fire was doused, the windows opened to let in fresh air, and everything was back to normal, I hugged Juneau tightly and told her how much I loved her. I also told her she was a hero, but her only response was a wagging tail and a sloppy kiss.

For years there was a nightly ritual, which unfolded at dusk, summer and winter. As the skies darkened Juneau started to pace, responding to some inner force over which she had no control. Her restless wandering persisted until the door was opened and she was able to escape into the night.

Through the window her dark shape could be seen outlined on the grass, silent and still as she listened intently for sounds of life and movement among the nocturnal creatures hidden in the undergrowth. True to her Arctic heritage, deep snow and sub-zero weather only seemed to enhance her desire for the cold outside world, but before midnight she could be found standing by the back door, at peace with herself and ready to rejoin the only family she had ever known. When early morning came she was content to sleep, occasionally twitching and snuffling as she played out her dreams of some imaginary chase.

I always felt that Juneau knew, in her own way, that any kind of hunting was strictly off-limits in our household, but many times instinct was a driving force too powerful for her to resist. That she also knew she had me to contend with was made very clear by the way she squinted at me out of the corner of her eye when she gave chase to a rabbit or squirrel as she tried to make her catch. She was expert at finding rodents in the long grass, but sometimes I was close enough to intercede. On those occasions she calmly surrendered, allowing me to open her mouth, recover her prize and set it free. Except for the bird-hunting cats, which occasionally invaded our property, she was never a threat to either humans or domestic animals.

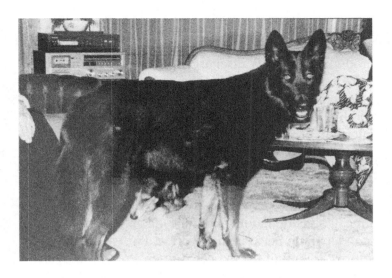

When Juneau was four years old I did something I had never done before—and would never do again. I allowed her to mate. The decision was against my better judgment, and I had some misgiving which later proved to be well founded, but I conceded to circumstances that seemed to be right at the time.

Juneau had first come into heat at two years of age, average for wild wolves. Our male dogs were neutered and all fences on the property were high enough to prevent canine outsiders from penetrating our stronghold and, although I firmly believe in spaying and neutering for domestic pets, I couldn't help but feel that spaying was an affront to Juneau's natural dignity. At that time I was reluctant to impose it upon her.

The following year, when it came that time again, she restlessly roamed house and garden, sniffing and searching. She remained in heat much longer than

I had anticipated. In her fourth year she became "interesting" many weeks earlier than expected, producing a bloody discharge long before estrus. After some research I found that this is not abnormal for a lone female wolf seeking a male partner in the wild, and by her behavior I knew that Juneau, too, was intensely occupied in finding a mate.

One of our friends, Steve, had a strikingly handsome long-haired German Shepherd with an impressive pedigree, that was originally imported from Germany. Steve, who had always been captivated by Juneau's gentle nature and majestic appearance, now urged a union between my wolf and his shepherd in return for pick of the expected litter. Pressured by my friend — and by Juneau — I finally gave in. Both Steve and Juneau were delighted.

At the appointed time, five wolf-hybrid pups were born in early spring at the back of my walk-in clothes closet. As the Colorado weather was still bitterly cold, Peter had built a comfortable den for her at the back of the spacious enclosure and Juneau was happy to let her human family visit and handle her babies as often as necessary. She was an excellent mother.

When they were old enough to be dispersed to different homes, one beautiful little black female went to live with Steve and his family and her German shepherd father. The wife named her "Tundra" for her Alaskan heritage, and she became Steve's pride and joy. A very large male went to a good friend who lived in the wilds of Montana, and one (named "Mischa" by Susie) remained with us. Mother and daughter formed a close bond, and I was always glad that Juneau had one of her own offspring with her for the rest of her life.

A young married couple happened to hear about Juneau and her pups. They contacted me and asked if they could see the two remaining members of the litter, one male and one female. I brought the pair downstairs and the young man and his wife fell in love with them immediately. They sat on the floor of our living room, holding the puppies and playing with them, while I carefully explained what the future would bring: the two small, adorable babies would soon be large wolf hybrids. At great length I counseled them on care and treatment so that the adoptees would remain gentle and friendly in adulthood. I stressed the importance of having them live in the house as "family" and the benefits of frequent handling and petting.

The husband told me they were building a home in the country with several acres of ground where the pups could have a lot of freedom. Both he and his wife seemed to be quite knowledgeable about rearing young animals, and talked about the horses they planned to buy so they could live a truly western outdoor life. Finally, after several hours, they disappeared in an expensive automobile, the wife happily clutching two little hybrid wolves.

Before leaving, every adopter of each of the four pups signed a notarized form ensuring a good home for life, no chaining, and a stipulation that if not completely satisfied with the new member of the family it (or they) would be returned to me immediately. I was convinced that all the puppies had above average homes, and now that her natural urges had been satisfied — and despite my previous reluctance — Juneau was spayed.

The years passed, and in the early days many of our walks took us through marshy ground where wild ducks made their home, and it was here that an incident took place which was almost humorous in retrospect. One cold winter's day Juneau stalked a Mallard duck as it floated serenely and unsuspectingly near the reeds that bordered the water on a pond. Neither the duck nor I recognized Juneau's stealthy approach until it was too late, but as she made her final burst of speed I, too, sprang into action. Luckily the duck was strong, and as Juneau battled with flapping wings and flailing legs I charged down the bank, yelling at the top of my voice. I grabbed Juneau's tail with one hand and an ear in the other, and the three of us became a writhing, squawking mass of fur and feathers in the icy water. I shifted my hand from her ear to cover her nose with my free hand, and instinctively her mouth opened wide as she gasped for air. Instantly, the duck rose into the misty realms above us and with indignant squawks flew off into the distance, completely unscathed. Now the excitement of the moment was over Juneau's head lowered and her tail drooped in shame as I angrily scolded her, both of us covered with mud and a sprinkling of feathers in the frigid water. But within minutes she was forging ahead, the whole incident forgotten as she hunted for field mice in the long grass.

One strange characteristic was her fascination with birds on the wing. I had never observed this trait in the many dogs that had shared my life over the years. Her eyes would trace movements of the sparrows as they flitted about the garden, hawks hovering in search of prey, or swallows darting overhead. When Canada geese streamed through the western skies, honking high above us, Juneau would point her nose heavenward to follow their flight until the last feathered member of the convoy disappeared from view. Her uniqueness was always a source of wonder and delight to those of us who knew and loved her.

But that was all many years ago. Now in her fourteenth year, her gait is slower and broad-based. The yellow eyes which once detected small movements half a mile away are dimmer; the nose is just as keen, but the ears which could have heard the proverbial pin drop in the next room are dulled with age. Although her fur is still thick and luxuriant, her muzzle is white and the bushy tail is laced with gray. The squirrels in the backyard are safe now as Juneau lies in the sun, watching them through half-closed eyes, too stiff for the chase.

After she is gone, I will remember Juneau on fall days when the mountain air is cool and crisp, and the clumps of aspen turn to brilliant canopies of red-gold. A special moment in time, which remains imprinted on my memory, was on just such a day as we climbed in the high country. Sam, my sweet and gentle Borzoi, was trotting ahead. Although a direct descendant of generations of wolfhounds purposely bred to chase down and kill the magnificent Russian wolf, Sam never hunted. Jenny, our feisty little sheepdog, was on some special mission of her own, and Juneau was exploring a wooded area more than a hundred yards away. Suddenly the trail we had been following became treacherous. As I inadvertently stepped on some loose rocks I lost my balance and, unable to keep my footing, I slid down a steep incline on my back. For a few moments I lay motionless, stunned by the force of my fall. Almost before my undignified descent had come to a halt, Juneau appeared, swiftly and silently out of nowhere. As she stood protectively over me, nose scenting the air and eyes scanning every direction for possible danger, I experienced an indescribable sense of safety. Like a sentinel on duty, rigid and alert, she stood guard over me until I struggled painfully to my feet. Then she was off again like the wind, happily investigating every little scent that wafted to her keen nostrils. Sam and Jenny stood at the bottom of the incline, gazing in mild surprise as they wondered what had happened. But Juneau knew.

After she is gone I will remember her fleeting across meadows, joyously free, poetry in motion, but always keenly aware of my presence. If she strayed briefly out of sight her head was soon visible, rising up from the undergrowth or silhouetted against the mountain backdrop, carefully keeping track of all my movements. To her I have always been the alpha, the leader of the pack who must be respected and obeyed.

She still looks magnificent, proud and independent despite the inevitable aging. And again questions flood my mind, this time accompanied by memories both sweet and poignant. If she goes before I do, what will it be like without her warm body pressed close against mine each day, squeezed between my knees and the counter as I prepare her evening meal? How will I fill the empty void in the quiet of the night when she is no longer lying by my side, her regular breathing an assurance of protection and safety?

She continues to make her nightly rounds, padding from room to room, as though to satisfy herself that family members are safely tucked in their beds before she retires to her own chosen spot by my side. There will be sadness and heartaches when she is no longer there to carry out her self-appointed tasks. As for myself, perhaps most of all I will miss the music of her voice - the haunting wolf call which is her one contribution to the wild she never knew. I will miss Juneau my gentle, beautiful wolf more than words can tell.

Juneau's story was written several months before her death, and is a tribute to a very special member of our family circle. Juneau died peacefully in my arms on a warm June evening at the age of fourteen years and five months. Her ashes rest in a brightly colored little box on the sun porch where she loved to lie.

CODY AND CHINOOK

Cody and Chinook were brother and sister awaiting euthanization when I received the call. It was at the height of the wolf craze when many people considered it a status symbol to "own" one of these magnificent animals. Some regarded it as neat to have a half-wild creature in their backyard, and there were others who just loved them for themselves. But the backyard breeders were there, indiscriminately turning out litters of wolf hybrids for profit, and in some cases even pure wolves were bred and sold illegally. It is a sad reality that many of these animals were shamefully treated, with scores of them confined to small enclosures or chained in yards, deprived of much human contact. Others were beaten into submission when undesirable wolf traits surfaced. Soon shelters were filled with hybrids when people who had purchased them as cute pups found they were unable or unwilling to cope with mature, half wild wolf-dogs.

Unfortunately the lack of fear acquired from the dog parent, together with basic wolf instincts and poor management, often formed a dangerous combination, which led to tragic consequences. As a result, humane societies and the regular cat and dog shelters were reluctant to place high-percentage wolf hybrids up for adoption. The quickest and safest solution was euthanasia.

A friend of ours who worked at one of the local shelters made the call. She already knew we had a wolf, a needy female we had adopted earlier, and had seen the close relationship develop between the wolf, Juneau, and my family. This lady desperately wanted to save the two siblings who were hours away from death, so talking fast and with obvious concern, she came straight to the point.

"Two hybrid wolves were brought in this morning," she said. "They are brother and sister, and about fifty percent wolf, so they are going to be destroyed today. Is there any way you can help?"

Noting the urgency in her voice, I realized there was no time to lose. Jim was at work, and after a brief telephone call it was decided that we would try to do something, even if it was only to offer a temporary refuge until a permanent solution could be found. I called my friend back. "I'll be there in thirty minutes," I told her.

The two hybrids were together in a pen, huddled in one corner, and despite their heartbreaking appearance I recognized them at once. The image of two enchanting little pups born at the back of my clothes closet flashed across my mind, and I felt a surge of rage and disgust, mingled with a strong sense of personal guilt.

They were a pathetic sight. Their necks were rubbed raw where heavy chain collars had dug deeply into the flesh. Their pads were cracked and worn down, suggesting that at some time they had been chained for long periods on hot concrete. In addition, their coats, which should have been thickly furred at that time of year, were thin and poor from under-nourishment. When I approached them with my friend they both came up to us, hindquarters low to the ground, tails sweeping the concrete floor with tentative wags.

At home there was a very large pen, an enclosure seldom used but excellent for an animal emergency such as this. At one end of the large dog run was a wooden hut separated into two sleeping quarters by a low divider and with overhead lights designed to heat the building in winter. Surrounding the whole area a double link chain fence, ten feet high and reinforced at the bottom with concrete, was sturdy enough to thwart any attempts at escape, so I knew the two hybrids would be safe there.

After receiving the necessary permission from the shelter manager and filling in numerous forms, my friend and I easily loaded them into the back of my pickup truck. Jim, who had purposely left work early, met me as I drove into the yard with two very subdued wolf hybrids, and together we put them into the enclosure and brought them food and water. We were relieved to find them very friendly, squatting on the ground in front of us to be petted.

Beside me I could hear Jim as he stroked their heads. "If I knew where those two idiots were I'd knock their damn heads together," he was muttering angrily, "and they'd be lucky if that's all I did."

So here we were with Cody and Chinook (named by me), two eighteen-month-old hybrid wolves and a big problem! We already had two dogs plus a hybrid that was only a hairs breadth away from pure Arctic tundra wolf. This was our beloved Juneau, a sweet and gentle creature who was the descendant of a union between an errant male sled dog and a wild wolf many years before. A needy, ninety-four percent little wolf pup, she came to us at the beginning of the craze that was sweeping the state. She had now been with us for several years and was a cherished member of our family. In addition, one of our dogs was Sam, a large Russian Wolfhound, thus it was doubtful if we would be able to keep Cody. Having already experienced the male alpha syndrome with Tim, there was no way I was going to put up with that kind of situation again. I never suspected that I was about to experience the female alpha syndrome.

Juneau and Mischa accepted the pair, as they accepted all newcomers, and there was no sign of recognition on either side. Even though Cody was in such poor condition he was young and strong, and we knew that with care he would soon recover. Chinook, although the same age, was in a much worse state than her brother and was going to need more concentrated nursing before she regained her health and strength.

We decided that she should remain with us at least until she was well again. We also entertained the idea that this could be her permanent home.

I hesitated about separating brother and sister, but they did not seem to be particularly attached to each other. In fact, Chinook frequently tried to dominate her bigger and more powerful brother with typical wolf behavior. He always submitted with good grace, so we failed to recognize this as anything more ominous than normal sibling horseplay. When Cody was adopted into what we knew would be an excellent home in the mountains with a friend who was well acquainted with wolf lore, Chinook didn't even seem to notice he was gone. The latest picture I have of Cody, taken a couple of years after he left us, shows a handsome wolf-dog in the back of an open jeep, tongue hanging out and what looks like a very happy smile on his face!

After Cody was gone we started bringing Chinook into the house so she would not have to stay alone in the enclosure. At first she was a model of good conduct. She got along well with Sam, the majestic, honey-colored Borzoi, and there was a relaxed friendliness with Mischa, her sister, as they played together on the lawn. But with Juneau, Chinook deferred to the older wolf with reluctance and a glint in her yellow eyes. Then, as she approached two years of age, her attitude changed — a fact we noted but did not take seriously enough at the time. She had almost reached maturity and was starting to challenge Juneau openly for leadership of the "pack," even though the latter had never made any attempt to dominate. Juneau had always been perfectly at ease with the other animals and had remained gentle and affectionate throughout all the years with us. Nonetheless, in spite of the older wolf's reluctance to be goaded into a confrontation, Chinook started shouldering her, determined to block her passage if she tried to reach Jim or me. Sometimes she walked around Juneau stiff-legged and growling, hackles raised, daring her to move.

Jim and I discussed this change in behavior, remembering the aggressive horseplay Chinook had exhibited with her brother. We both agreed it was time for her to move on before she caused serious problems with Juneau. We thought of several options but we were too late. Before we could put any plan into action they had their first fight.

One day, without warning, Chinook attacked. I was in the yard with them when it happened and was totally unprepared for what was about to take place. Juneau was seven years old and her advancing age and mild disposition gave Chinook, now reaching her prime, a distinct advantage. For a female, Juneau was an unusually big wolf, weighing almost ninety pounds. Chinook was smaller, but a lithe, sinewy body and muscles of steel compensated for what she lacked in size. As she struck Juneau with full force the wolf, taken by surprise, fell on her side. Within seconds she was on her feet again, ready to meet the challenge, and with tail up and head down, she seized Chinook by the throat. This gave Chinook the perfect opening and she grabbed Juneau's head, tearing the scalp from ear to ear. Juneau thrust for the underbelly, but by this time I had managed to reach the garden hose and turned it on with full force. The stream of water knocked them apart, and before Chinook could attack again I directed a powerful jet stream onto her face and shoulders. She retreated into the pen, leaving a bleeding Juneau outside. I slammed the gate shut and Juneau was rushed to a veterinarian with an ice pack on her head to stem the bleeding and preserve the lacerated, semi-detached scalp. This was skillfully sewn back together again and healed completely, leaving no evidence of the unprovoked attack.

Chinook was banished permanently to the outside enclosure while we contemplated the situation and our next plan of action. It was obvious that she and Juneau could never be together again, and keeping them totally segregated was going to be a monumental chore. We didn't want to resort to having Chinook put down, but finding a home for her with someone who might not be able to manage her humanely was also out of the question. The fact that she was sweet and loving with people and had gotten along well with dogs influenced our decision to try other solutions. A week went by and then the whole problem was inadvertently resolved. I made a deadly mistake.

I had left Chinook on the sun porch, which was separated from the living room by a door and a large glass window. Juneau lay peacefully in the living room, either unaware or unconcerned that Chinook was only a few yards away on the porch. I was in the process of getting a leash, preparing to take Chinook for an evening walk when there was a sudden crash of breaking glass. I was transfixed with horror as a ball of fury and hatred came hurtling through the shattered window, straight at Juneau.

A death struggle between two powerful animals with the blood and instincts of a wolf is an awesome and terrifying sight. All the primeval forces lying just below the surface burst through in a relentless urge to kill. As Chinook went for the throat Juneau grabbed a foreleg in an effort to break it, and when Chinook wrenched her leg away Juneau lunged for the throat. Then she swiftly pivoted, and using her forelegs she mounted Chinook's back in a grim struggle to break her adversary's neck. Chinook, twisting her body and head, seized Juneau by the throat and when Juneau broke away the hybrid tore hair and skin from the underbelly. As her back was now exposed Juneau again mounted her, opening up a large gash as she attempted to break the spine. Bodies locked together, they became one frenzied mass of bloody flesh and bone on the living room floor. Juneau held her own and was able to meet the challenge of her much younger opponent, but clearly this was a fight to the death and I knew Chinook could be the victor.

Mercifully, Jim was upstairs and heard the violent struggle as well as my frantic screams for help. Running down the stairs two at a time he grabbed the nearest tail, which happened to be Juneau's. On the other side of the melee I tried to do the same with Chinook, but it was a few precious moments before I managed to capture her flailing extremity. With both of them snarling, huge fangs exposed as they lunged for each others' throats, I shuffled backwards, dragging Chinook by the tail, through the dining room and kitchen to the back porch. Jim followed, ready to close the kitchen door, and clutching Juneau's tail in a vice-like grip as she struggled to reach Chinook, bent on continuing the gory battle now that it had started.

After what seemed like an eternity I made it to the back door, Chinook still fighting like a demented creature as she plunged again and again in the direction of Juneau and Jim. As the two of us disappeared down the outer steps to the patio, Jim slammed the door, shutting us both outside and corralling Juneau in the kitchen.

It was not until later, when we both collapsed on to the sofa, shaking and emotionally drained, that we took in the enormity of the situation. Two enraged wolves in mortal combat, dragged apart by their tails! I sent up a silent prayer of thanks that we had both come through the ordeal unscathed. But it was the end of the line for Chinook.

I sent an urgent SOS over the telephone to Peter, our son, who fortunately lived close by, and the three of us took two deflated combatants, both of them bleeding profusely, to an animal emergency room to be cleaned up and stitched back together. By this time both were quiet and docile, but we were taking no chances. They traveled in separate vehicles, securely leashed, bandaged and subdued.

As soon as we arrived home I made an urgent call to a no-kill rescue group some fifty miles away. I had previously met the owner and knew he took in all types of needy animals, especially dogs and wolf hybrids. Yes, they would take Chinook as soon as her wounds healed.

Chinook was again relegated to the pen outside and both she and Juneau recovered surprisingly quickly, with no permanent damage, and only a few scars on Juneau to remind us of our "wild child," Chinook.

Soon the day came for Chinook to leave. I took her out to the refuge, which was a sprawling assembly of huts and large runs on many acres of prairie that housed several hundred animals. They all looked well fed and well cared for, and I noticed a little retinue of dogs following the owner when he came to greet me.

The wolf-hybrids were housed in a separate area from the dogs, with roomy pens and platforms high off the ground where many of them were resting. Although this might not be the best solution for Chinook the only alternative was euthanization, which I felt should be a last resort. But when he learned that she was accustomed to living in the house, was affectionate with humans and had shown no aggressive tendencies towards dogs, the owner decided that she would be kept separate from the other wolf-dogs. She would have much more freedom to roam, and if she behaved herself she could earn the privilege of sleeping in the house with him and several of his companion dogs. He seemed perfectly comfortable with her previous behavior, and obviously had a great deal of experience with both wild and domestic animals. I gave Chinook a hug, wished her well, and shed a few tears as I drove away.

About a month later I drove out to the sanctuary to see how my "wild child" was doing. As I passed through the gates the owner was making his rounds with the same little band of dogs following behind. To my great surprise Chinook was at the head of the pack. As I watched the procession from my truck I saw her block one dog, apparently for some minor infringement of pack etiquette. As she stood over him menacingly he sank to the ground in total submission, then they both companionably trotted on together, Chinook taking her place again at the head of the column. I knew then that she had found her niche in life and was happy. She was the leader of the pack, in total control, and had at last attained the goal she had struggled for most of her life.

Chinook died at the age of nine from an undiagnosed case of hypothyroidism. Despite my sadness when I heard the news, I was consoled by the knowledge that for those few years she had been content, fulfilling her one ambition in life. Chinook was the alpha female — even if her "pack" was only a small collection of domesticated dogs!

BILLY

The first time I saw Billy he was a roly-poly little puppy playing by himself in a very large garden, happily chasing leaves on a warm spring day. As I watched him, he paused to whirl around in a wild effort to catch his own tail, which stayed just out of reach. After several fruitless gyrations he plopped down on a bed of leaves, a picture of pleasant relaxation. I was on my way to work at the time and running late, but I couldn't help slowing down to take a peek at this cute baby with his gray furry body and paws that seemed too big for him as he sat panting on the lawn.

I was at a stoplight so had a few moments to enjoy his playful antics before I noticed an unsavory-looking character with dirty clothes and long, unkempt hair walking past the fence where the puppy was now rolling delightedly back and forth in the grass. As I watched, I saw the man stop and furtively fumble with the garden gate while stretching his hand out towards the little dog. I was on the same side of the street and through my open truck window I could hear him calling softly: "Come here, fella. Come here, boy."

At the other side of the fence the puppy looked up inquiringly and then started towards the now open gate. The man walked on slowly, turning his head as he snapped his fingers at the small figure that ambled out of the garden and followed him down the street. By this time I was beginning to have the uncomfortable feeling that the man was a predator and I lingered, wondering whether I should follow them. The blast of a horn behind me and the sight of an angry face in my rearview mirror energized me to move forward. I accelerated through the intersection and was forced to continue on down the road as the man and small dog turned down an alley behind me. I was still wondering what I could have said had I approached the suspected dognapper. I could have asked sternly if the puppy belonged to him and risk being told to mind my own business. Or I could just ignore the bad vibes that I was acutely feeling and forget the whole thing. At the time I had no proof that this questionable-looking character was actually trying to steal the puppy and my instincts told me to drive on. Then my conscience dictated that I risk being nosy, and also extremely late for work. As there was no place to park I turned right at the next light, intending to circle the block and meet the pair at the other end of the street where they had disappeared. To my intense frustration I was met by another one-way street and by the time I had maneuvered my way through a maze of streets and alleys they had both vanished.

The uneasy feeling I was experiencing turned to genuine concern but I had no choice other than to drive on. All day long I was haunted by the thought of a potential dog-napping, and when I got home that evening I couldn't wait to tell my husband what I had seen and what I suspected. I had already anticipated a male reaction telling me to stop worrying about something I couldn't do anything about, and Jim lived up to my expectations.

"Why are you getting yourself all upset, honey? There was nothing you could do. And you don't even know if he was stealing."

I knew he was right, but for the next few days I scanned the Lost and Found column of all the newspapers in the area. Within a week I had found a few paragraphs describing a lost puppy. It gave the address where I had watched the little dog playing only a few days before, and I knew at once that my suspicions were correct. I called the phone number published in the paper and talked to a very distressed woman. She told me that the missing puppy was a three-month-old Siberian Husky named Billy, and that she was caring for him while his family was on vacation. I described to her what I had seen, which included the suspicious-looking character and the street where they had both vanished. The poor lady was so distraught; and for some reason I was feeling such an overwhelming sense of guilt that I offered to help her find Billy. I was convinced that I should have been able to prevent a clear case of dog-napping, even though that was a totally unreasonable assumption on my part.

Billy had disappeared from a small community of about fifteen hundred people, so there was a chance that someone might recognize him from the picture on the "Dog Missing" posters that were duly attached to boards and telephone poles. The distraught dog-sitter promised to search the streets for him and put up the posters, in addition to the unpleasant task of informing her friends that she had lost their dog.

Weeks turned into months with no news of the missing puppy. His family had returned from a vacation in Europe and was devastated by the news.

They posted offers of a large reward, but by this time it seemed Billy had vanished into thin air.

The correctional facility to which I traveled each day was situated in the country, not far from the little town where Billy was last seen. As I drove down the dusty main street each morning I was constantly scanning the front yard of every house I passed and scrutinizing each dog that came into view. In the evening after work I detoured through the alleys and made frequent stops to peer at anyone who looked suspiciously furtive and scruffy enough to be a dognapper. I often stopped at the one small grocery store in town to talk to Randy, the owner, who appeared to know everyone, both in town and in the surrounding country. He always brought me up to date on all the local news, which, to my disappointment, never included sightings of a stray puppy.

Then one day I got an unexpected break. It was now late summer, and I happened to stop at the store on my way home. As I lingered to make a purchase the local sheriff came in and started talking to Randy. As they casually chatted I overheard the officer say that a young dog had been hanging around the cookhouse of the minimum security prison for several weeks and some of the inmates had taken pity on him. They had been feeding him on the quiet and then a few days ago the dog suddenly disappeared. I pricked up my ears (figuratively speaking) and moved closer so that I could eavesdrop on the conversation.

"He was there, off and on, until a few days ago" the sheriff said, "and then he was gone."

"What did he look like?" Randy queried.

"All I know is what I heard. I guess this dog looks about eight or nine months old, a fairly big guy, bushy gray coat, looked kinda like a wolf," replied the officer. "Trouble is there's been talk of some of the livestock around here being killed. Dan up on the mesa lost some chickens, and one of his dogs was beat up last night. He reported it to me and that's what I'm doing now. Making inquiries. Trying to get some information."

"It could'a bin coyotes," offered Randy as he bagged some groceries.

The sheriff stood at the counter, ruminating. "Coulda' bin," he finally agreed, "But we need to find this dog and get rid of it. When I have time I'll round up Dan, and maybe some of the other guys, and we'll go on a little hunting trip."

From this conversation I knew what "a little hunting trip" meant. Men would go out with guns and, innocent or guilty, the dog would be shot. The sheriff had described a dog similar to the stolen puppy, which would now be about eight months old, and I was more convinced than ever that this could be Billy. Feeling that I had a personal stake in his survival and propelled by the urgency of the situation, I exited the store as soon as possible. I needed to plan a rescue operation.

It was late afternoon and there was no chance that I could set off on my own on what would probably end up to be a wild goose chase in the dark. I headed for home, but I couldn't forget the conversation and the young dog that was homeless through no fault of his own. I remembered the cute little pup happily playing by himself in the leaves, and wondered what had happened to him in the months that followed. Clearly he was stolen from a caring family, and now he was going to be hunted down and shot. I very much doubted that he was responsible for dead chickens, and I didn't believe he was old enough or strong enough to "beat up" a farm dog. I had to find him.

As soon as I reached home I started making plans, and the next day I made my way to the minimum-security prison, which was in a different complex but within walking distance of my office. As a prison employee I had no difficulty getting in. It was lunch time and the dining room was full so I stopped to talk to some of the inmates and then the prison cooks. They all seemed to know about the young dog and were eager to talk. I got a good description and was now more convinced than ever that it was Billy.

The following day was a Saturday, so I enlisted Jim's help and we set off together at dawn. Within an hour we had passed through the dusty little town where I had first seen Billy and were out on the open plains. I figured that the dog, if it was still alive, would not be far away as it had spent so much time around the prison. Jim was driving my pickup truck so we were able to cover the rough territory fairly easily, although in places the ride was bumpy and uncomfortable. We drove around scanning the open country with field glasses, but all we saw was a lone coyote and later a golden eagle soaring in the sky. As we traveled on we came across a herd of pronghorns grazing, and another coyote hunting beside a stream. Normally, we would have stopped the truck to enjoy the early morning beauty surrounding us, but this time we were trying to beat a posse that undoubtedly would take advantage of the weekend to do their hunting.

We covered many miles, crossing and re-crossing tracks where cattle and wildlife made their daily pilgrimage in search of food and water. We explored a mesa and cliffs where Billy might have found shelter, but could detect no signs of life beyond a few scurrying rodents.

It was noon when we saw a gray, wolf-like figure crossing a patch of open ground, heading for a jumble of rocks and cave-like indentations on a shallow hillside. Instead of the tail curled over the back, as one would have expected in a Husky, it was carried straight out behind, giving a streamlined effect. When the animal paused the bushy tail hung straight down between the hind legs, presenting a wolfish appearance. It was about a hundred yards away and Jim accelerated, bumping over the uneven ground in an attempt to head it off. It paused for a moment to look at us, and then started to run. Before the animal could reach the shelter of the rocks we were in front of it, and saw at close quarters a scrawny half-grown Husky pup. I now knew without a doubt that this was the dog we were looking for.

We had brought food with us, including meat to entice Billy in case we were lucky enough to find him, but the dog now doubled back, heading for open country, All hope of using meat as bait was gone. Jim reversed and we set off in hot pursuit. Billy coursed from side to side, making it difficult for us to keep up with him in case lest dog was run down by the bumping pickup, which alternately flew up in the air or dropped abruptly into a depression in the ground.

After almost a mile of full flight Billy started to tire. His gait became weary and he slowed to a trot. Wherever he turned Jim was close behind him until finally, sides heaving, tongue hanging out, Billy dropped to the ground. It was a pathetic sight, and one we would have gladly foregone, but there was no other way.

Billy raised his head, turning it to watch us steadily with exquisite blue eyes as we slowly climbed out of the truck and approached him, as quietly and cautiously as possible. At first he made a heroic effort to get to his feet, but dropped back exhausted. We knelt beside him, talking gently and soothingly, until his initial fear subsided and he laid his head back on the ground. My husband got to his feet and went to the truck where he found the picnic hamper and poured ice- old bottled water into a bowl. Kneeling again, he held it in front of the dog. Billy lifted his head and drank thirstily. Then Jim poured some of the water onto a cloth and bathed Billy's head until the heaving chest quieted and breathing returned to normal. We could see the taut muscles starting to relax, even as he continued to keep a watchful eye on both of us. Finally his eyelids drooped and the body became limp as tension drained away.

Billy had a tight chain around his throat that had apparently never been changed to accommodate his growing neck, but this would have to do until we could get him home. I went to the truck for a leash and I also picked up the package of meat and brought it over to where Billy was still lying on the ground. Hesitantly, he smelled it and then hungrily began to devour it.

When the leash was clipped on to the chain collar and we rose to go, Billy followed us with tail drooping and head hanging low. Jim was cautious as he put both arms around the dog to lift him into the back of the pickup truck, but Billy submitted without a struggle. He lay on the blanket in the back of the truck, still plainly exhausted after his ordeal, and it seemed as though he was even relieved to be taken care of at last.

After we arrived home and Billy was safely installed in a room away from all our other dogs, I went to phone the dog-sitter who had been so devastated when he disappeared. She had given up the search a few weeks after he was gone, but we had kept in touch, and now I wanted her to hear the good news as soon as possible. When I told her excitedly that Billy had finally been found and could return to his family at once, she hesitated. I wondered why she didn't share my enthusiasm, and then she explained. She said that she was surprised and pleased he had been rescued but his family had just adopted another Husky puppy and she didn't think they would want to take on a second dog. She told me that she would get in touch with them and let them know where Billy was, but apparently she was right. They didn't want him back.

So Billy now had his "forever home" with us, together with three other dogs. Like all our canines he was neutered immediately, and settled in quite happily to family life, but for us "family life" became far more complicated. Billy had been on his own long enough that some of the wild spirit he had acquired during that time caused instant problems in a reasonably orderly household. If he had been potty trained in his early days he'd forgotten all he was taught, and any place in the house became his own personal toilet. He ran through the rooms, knocking over flower arrangements, furniture, or anything in his path, and pushed past anyone who tried to open a door. He scratched feverishly at entrances when he wanted to come in, ruining wood and paint, and in addition to his other lapses in good manners Billy was a thief! Within days he had found that by standing on his hind legs he could reach the top of the dining room table or kitchen counter and nothing edible could be left unguarded.

On the positive side, once he had accommodated to civilized life again he turned out to be a happy-go-lucky, good-natured young dog that loved to play and responded to chest rubs, petting and hugging with wriggles of joy. On the negative side, his own idea of affection was to leap joyfully on anyone who happened to be near, putting his big paws on their chest in a frantic effort to plant sloppy kisses on neck and face.

At that time my schedule did not allow for intensive doggy training so I started scouting around for someone who would be willing to undertake that task. I finally found an elderly retired college professor who had trained dogs in his younger days and was interested in taking on the challenge of socializing our young delinquent. At first he came to our home so that he and Billy could become acquainted, and then started training him in earnest.

Bob was a patient, experienced trainer and by the time Billy was fourteen months old he had become a different dog. Bob found him to be intelligent and a quick learner, and from the start they formed an alliance that enabled them to work well together. Billy soon graduated from simple commands like "Sit", "Stay", and "Lie down" to more advanced training. He learned to come immediately when called, leaving behind tantalizing smells in instant obedience, and within a few months he was walking at heel without a leash, or waiting patiently in one spot until told he could move.

I was equally pleased with his progress in the home. He became an obedient and loving member of the family and a pleasure to be around. There were no more messes in corners or on carpets, and he was able to walk calmly through the house instead of indulging in the wild cavalry charges that previously left the place a shambles. He no longer stood on his hind legs to greet people with such abandon that they lost their balance and were in danger of falling over backwards. Instead, he greeted them decorously with gentle blue eyes and sweeping wags of his beautiful long tail. He still helped himself to anything on the kitchen counter or the dining room table when we were not looking, and neither Jim nor I could break him of the habit. However, considering the tremendous progress he had made, (and since there was nothing we could do about it anyway) I managed to persuade myself that this was only a slight misdemeanor.

Billy lived to be a very old dog and was sadly missed when he finally passed on.

MAX II

When I was growing up in England, many years ago, all of my dogs were sheepdogs, born on surrounding farms to patients of my country doctor father. One of my most faithful companions was an Old English Sheepdog named Max. Max traveled everywhere with me — on trains, buses, into restaurants, and sometimes on special occasions to tea parties hosted by my mother or her friends. In those days there were no laws barring well-behaved dogs from accompanying their "special person" to a restaurant or café, and a familiar sight was a farmer or shepherd enjoying a pint of beer in the local pub with his dogs lying at his feet. Even now, in the Yorkshire dales, one can sometimes see a working sheepdog lying under the bar or beside her master, both relaxing as he sips his glass of ale.

At the age of ten, to my indescribable delight I was given my very own puppy, separate from the family dogs that everyone claimed as their own. When it came time to find a name for the new arrival, within approximately two minutes from the time I first held the squirming puppy in my arms, I asked my father to do the honors. He chose the name "Max." No one knew why he selected this masculine title for such an obviously feminine little ball of fluff, and strangely enough no one ever thought to ask. There was another slight deviation from the norm that no one ever quite figured out — for the whole thirteen years of her life my father always referred to Max as "he," even though she gave birth to two litters of puppies over the years. I can only think that this harmless peculiarity stemmed from a preference for male dogs and that father stubbornly refused to acknowledge her feminine gender. So "Max" she remained, and was awarded the privilege of lying beside fathers chair at mealtimes so that he could surreptitiously drop little bites of food in her direction. This was a practice strictly forbidden for the rest of the family, so my patient mother just pretended not to notice.

By the end of the twentieth century I had called America my home for over forty years. Jim had been gone almost a year, succumbing to cancer, and the dogs we had loved and cared for together had all grown old and died. Mischa, our beautiful German Shepherd/wolf cross, also a victim of short-lived, incurable cancer, had been transported to the happy hunting grounds four months after Jim passed away, and Juneau, my beloved Arctic tundra wolf was nearly fourteen years old. She accepted Mischa's death phlegmatically, but it was obvious that she missed her. I believe animals understand and accept the concept of death, perhaps better than most humans, so I let her see and smell Mischa's body, hoping it would provide some sort of closure for her. I am sure it did because she never looked for Mischa again. She remained subdued, however, and sometimes appeared slightly despondent, lying quietly with head resting on paws. All her life she had been accustomed to a lively household as "rescues" constantly appeared, eventually growing old and dying, but there were always others to take their place. The house was unnaturally quiet now, which seemed to affect Juneau's normally upbeat nature, as it did mine. Besides, we both missed Jim.

It was then that the first puppy in years joined our family of two. He was not a rescue. When I first saw him he was a little figure standing forlornly by himself in a large dog run at the boarding and breeding kennels where he was born. Coming from a long line of champions, the cream of Old English Sheepdog aristocracy, his brothers and sisters undoubtedly were destined for fame and fortune on the show circuit. This lone puppy, born with a physical defect which necessitated early castration, would never see the inside of a show ring. Instead, he watched his siblings, all carefully chosen, be carried away one by one until he was the only occupant left in the enclosure.

He was ten weeks old at the time, still sporting the fluffy black and white coat he was born with, and which would soon turn to regulation gray and white. He had enormous paws and an engaging smile, and as he had no tail he waggled his little bottom from side to side in an ecstasy of delight when I reached through the wire to pet him.

Long ago I had made a pact with myself: I would only take elderly abused or neglected dogs that had never experienced love or kindness. Then, for the short time they had left, they would be showered with all the tenderness and affection they had never known. Up to that time I had clung to my self-imposed commitment, but now the sight and feel of this endearing little creature sabotaged all my altruistic resolutions. We went home together, and I named him "Max II" in loving memory of my first Old English Sheepdog.

    As I had already anticipated, Juneau welcomed Max II with motherly devotion. Within seconds she was sniffing him all over as he lay submissively on his back, all four paws in the air. Their affection for each other was consummated as she gave him a complete body wash, using her tongue to clean off all the lingering smells of breeding kennel life as diligently as if she had given birth to him herself. By evening he was her shadow. In the weeks that followed she patiently tolerated his sharp baby teeth when he hung from her bushy tail as she walked, his nose in her food bowl as she ate, and his body curled up against her as she slept. And as he grew she taught him to howl, wolf-style, every time an ambulance or fire truck passed the house, and sometimes just for the pure joy of howling. His voice didn't have quite the same timbre or ethereal enchantment as hers, but it could still be heard several blocks away.

Max's size increased rapidly until he far surpassed the average sheepdog. I attributed his huge size partly to wolf diet, as he shared Juneau's love of meat, which they both regularly inhaled with gusto. Although I personally detest the practice of killing, even for food, I was not prepared to infringe upon the laws of nature.

When Max was eight months old, Juneau passed on and we were again a household of two. By this time I was getting ready to retire from my job working in the prison system, and had decided, for the second time in my life, "No more rescues!" Max and I were going to live out the rest of our lives together in peace and harmony.

CHEYENNE AND ANDY

Max II was fifteen months old when the all too-familiar call came. This time a no-kill sanctuary was closing down and the animals were in desperate need. If homes were not found for them within a few days many of the older dogs were going to be euthanized by order of state authorities. A good Samaritan had taken it upon herself to call everyone she knew, and many she didn't.

"How many can you take? Two? Three?" she pleaded.

"None," I tried to say, but the word died on my lips.

Cheyenne and Andy arrived the following day. Cheyenne was a sweet-natured, homely looking mix of uncertain age and parentage. She was about the size of an English Springer Spaniel with short black hair and a stocky body rather reminiscent of a Rottweiler. Her upper lip was badly disfigured, probably the result of an attack by another dog, the wound neglected by her caregivers. This, unfortunately, gave her a permanently angry, even vicious, appearance that caused strangers to back off and give her a wide berth. It was obvious why she had never found a home.

My veterinarian, taking an educated guess, determined her to be eleven or twelve years old, perhaps older. Her eyes were clouding over, an unmistakable sign of advancing age, and like so many of the rescues that had been incarcerated for long periods of time, her teeth were badly broken where she had chewed on the wire in an effort to escape.

I came to love Cheyenne dearly, and spent many hours with her crouched across my lap as I tried to break through a mental barrier, a defense mechanism she had surrounded herself with, and which I was eventually able to penetrate. She was one of the most humble dogs I had ever known, quiet and self-effacing. When she first arrived she liked to be in dark corners, so I settled her in a wicker basket with a blanket and pillow in my bedroom closet. There she seemed to feel safe and was content to lie in semi-darkness for hours at a time.

After she had been with me for a few days I took Cheyenne for her first walk. She hung back on the leash, straining to return to the first real home she had known in years. I suspect she had never been walked before and her fears were painfully real; if she was taken away from one place it was to be discarded and then passed on to another strange and frightening place. She had never known the security of a permanent home or a family who cared about her. After a week or so she came to the realization that a walk meant only a temporary separation from her new home, and something to be enjoyed. Soon she was looking forward eagerly to her daily outings which involved walks in the park where there were all kinds of delightful smells, and rides on the front seat of the pickup truck where she could see everything that was going on in the world from her high perch.

A month passed and Cheyenne started to sneak out of the closet to be near me at night, so her basket was moved to my bedside. Soon she was on the bed, snuggling up to me as I slept. I was finally rewarded by seeing the dull, hopeless look that had engulfed her for so long replaced by an air of contentment and, when she knew something good was about to happen the eager light in her eyes would be accompanied by excited little dancing steps.

I only had my sweet Cheyenne for a year and six months before old age with its coexisting problems claimed her. It has been said that one year of human life is equivalent to seven doggy years, and I was grateful that I had been able to give her what were probably the happiest ten "dog years" of her life, and for that I felt truly blessed.

Andy was also eleven or twelve years old, and had shared accommodations with Cheyenne at the shelter. He was in poor condition when he first came to me and spent most of his time lying quietly near Cheyenne. He was golden-brown in color and medium in size, with soft hair that was badly matted when I first met him. He looked as if he might be a Shetland Sheepdog cross and, once he was bathed, groomed, and properly nourished, was strikingly handsome.

Andy had been bounced from home to home as a young dog, eventually ending up at the no-kill shelter where he had spent the next seven or eight years, living mostly an outdoor life in a pen with Cheyenne. The uncertainty of his early existence evidently took a toll because he was still suspicious and slow to make friends. He, too, was carrying some battle scars from previous altercations through the wire with dogs in neighboring pens, and he was missing several teeth. The teeth he still had were broken and discolored.

Although they had similar backgrounds, in temperament Andy was the exact opposite of Cheyenne. She was humble and retiring, ready to hide her head if anyone came too close, whereas Andy, as he recovered health and strength, was cocky and stood his ground. If I had to correct him for bad behavior, he was ready to fight. The second day after his arrival he messed in the middle of the living room carpet, staring me full in the face as though challenging me to utter one word of reproof. Knowing that he had spent most, if not all, of his life untrained in toilet etiquette, I was not surprised, but I did feel that this undesirable demonstration of bathroom behavior should be checked without delay. I pointed a finger towards the open back door, and fixing him with a stern look I told him "No, Andy. Outside." I moved towards him and instantly his upper lip curled. Directing a hostile glare towards me, he backed into a corner and gave a low growl. I decided that I would not press my luck and got to work with paper towels and sponges.

The next day the same thing happened. As he had just come in from the garden where I had spent ten minutes urging him to "be a good dog," and as the back door was still open, this was definitely adding insult to injury. I decided to take immediate action and advanced towards him, repeating, "No, Andy. Outside!" I was muttering under my breath, "You've just come in, you little monster. You are doing this to test me!"

Again I pointed to the open door and walked towards him, intending to take him by the collar and lead him outside. It was then that he rushed me, snarling as he hurled himself towards me with bared teeth. I knew he was not bluffing. I grabbed a chair, keeping it between us until he retreated behind the sofa, still growling ominously.

Just as disturbing to me was his attitude towards Max, which he constantly threatened with a show of yellow, broken teeth. A few years ago I would have regarded the situation as a challenge, but I had now reached the stage in life when I was not willing to put up with an aggressive, ill-tempered canine that was ready to attack me at the slightest provocation. Besides, Andy had resisted all my efforts to absorb him into the bosom of the family with kindness and treats.

After a week of Andy and his determined efforts to intimidate me, and the rest of the household, I decided I'd had enough. This uncouth little dog must go! I called the refuge that was still in the process of dispersing animals, and told them I was bringing Andy back. He was loaded into my pickup and deposited at the shelter with the genuine hope that he would find a home somewhere more to his liking. I knew the prospect was dim, but nevertheless I drove away feeling as if a very large, very disagreeable load had been catapulted from my shoulders.

Just a few days later I received a phone call and was surprised at what I heard. The person at the other end of the line informed me that Andy was behaving in a manner that was totally incompatible with his previous conduct at the shelter. In fact, the rather stern voice said, they had never seen him act like this in all the years he had spent with them. "He is digging at the fence, barking and howling all the time and biting at the wire. He is trying to get back to you," she intoned. "No one else wants him, and if you won't take him, he'll have to be destroyed."

I was astonished, and secretly flattered by the reception he gave me when I drove back again to pick him up and bring him home. He danced around me excitedly, jumping up and down, licking my hands and uttering little welcome noises. He tugged at the leash, pulling me towards my pickup truck. There was no doubt that Andy wanted to go home with me.

"You miserable old reprobate. One peep out of you and you're headed for the last roundup," I warned him. He looked up at me lovingly and wagged his tail.

When we got home he ran into the house excitedly. He even politely touched noses with Max, who didn't seem to be at all impressed. There were no more "accidents" in the house, and Andy was a model of decorum. For at least two weeks I didn't have to scold him for anything.

Then one morning I needed him to go outside with Max and Cheyenne, and he refused. He lowered his head, showing his teeth, newly cleaned and polished by the doggy doctor, and growled ominously. I'll try one more time, I thought, and if this doesn't work I'm through with this wretched little monster. Forever.

I went into the kitchen and opened the outside door wide. Then, making sure the door to the back porch and the door to the back garden were open, I put my plan into operation. I selected two large metal cooking pans and went to find Andy. He was lying complacently in the living room, no doubt congratulating himself on winning the first round and totally unaware of what was about to happen. I came to within a few inches of him and suddenly clashed the two pans together over his head, shrieking at the top of my voice, "Bad dog. Get out of here!"

As he fled out the door into the garden I stood on the doorstep, still clashing the pans together, which made a fearful sound, and shouting threats at him as he cowered by the garden gate. After two hours he was allowed back into the house, tail between legs, where he remained behind the couch for the rest of the day, subdued and crestfallen.

Andy never growled at me again. I was now top dog, and life vastly improved from that day on. If I said "Out," I had only to pick up a pan to have him scurry past me into the yard, and within days even a pan lid became a redundant resource. When I said "Andy, here" he came, and when I petted him he fawned over me. Like a child who is given boundaries, he seemed to appreciate the unaccustomed discipline. Although he never growled at me again, from time to time he still muttered harmless little obscenities at Max from a safe distance. Max completely ignored him.

The transformation was dramatic, but Andy's desire for intimacy developed gradually. The meanness and surly behavior that seemed to be such an integral part of his personality vanished with his last burst of anger and disobedience, but he was still slow to respond to the love I offered him. Previously he had tolerated petting and stroking, but had never sought it. As he became more compliant he received more caresses, and after a few weeks he responded to the increased attention with his own brand of affection. He started to follow me, upstairs and down, and when I bent to stroke him he licked my face and offered me a paw. If I was reading or watching television he would sit by my chair, leaning against my leg, and he became the official greeter at the front door when friends dropped in. Our affection for each other blossomed, and when I lost Cheyenne I slept pinned to the bed by Max on one side and Andy on the other.

Andy lived a happy three and a half years with us. When he was about fifteen he had difficulty climbing the stairs to my room, so towards the end I moved a fold-up cot into the living room to be near him; when he could no longer go for walks I lifted him into my pickup and drove him around so that he would have a change of scenery. He loved these outings and sat with nose pressed against the window, gazing out at the passing world. In the last days he became incontinent, so I covered the floors with plastic, and at the end, when the vet came to give him his last, lethal, injection, I held him in my arms and wept. Finally, overcome with sadness, I retreated into the kitchen, leaving him cuddled on Susie's lap until he drifted away to doggy heaven.

For many years I have accepted the harsh reality that the price you pay for taking old dogs, especially those that have had wretched lives, is the short time you have with them. The reward, however, substantially outweighs the pain. Just the fact that they died knowing that they were truly loved—probably for the first time in their lives—makes everything worthwhile.

MEG

News on the rescue grapevine travels fast, and it was not long after I lost Andy that the owner of a small animal refuge on the plains called me. He told me that his kennels were becoming overcrowded with dogs that had been thrown out of cars and left to die on the mesa by "owners" that had grown tired of them. Every day he scoured the surrounding areas for victims of this insane cruelty and the number of cats and dogs rescued was overwhelming him. He knew of Andy's passing, and asked if I would be willing to take an Australian Cattle Dog that had been picked up the previous year sitting beside a lonely track, miles away from the nearest highway.

When found, she had blood on her front paws and chin, suggesting a fall from a fast-moving vehicle, probably from the back of a pickup truck. She had no collar but she was friendly and well-nourished, and when she limped over to the rancher there was nothing to indicate that she had been intentionally abandoned or in any way abused. He had taken her to the refuge where they had posted notices locally, and efforts were made to find her "special person," but with no success. More than likely, her SP was already many miles away before he realized that she was missing, and a lost dog rarely stays in one place. When frantically searching for its family it can cover many miles in a comparatively short time. In rugged Colorado country, far from civilization, a lost or abandoned animal has little chance of survival. Death usually comes painfully from starvation or from mauling by hungry coyotes or mountain lions. Sometimes a pack of dogs will survive a short time by preying on livestock, but they are soon shot by ranchers protecting their herds.

This particular dog had been at the shelter for over six months, and although close confinement must have been especially trying for a healthy, active herding dog, at least her life had been spared. When the shelter owner called me I explained with great care that I now only took very elderly dogs, with the hope that their expectation of life was considerably shorter than mine. He told me that Meg had recently been examined by a veterinarian, who gave her approximate age as eight years; with this assurance in mind I agreed to meet with both of them and then make my decision.

They arrived that same day, and the moment he opened the door a ball of high-powered energy shot out of his truck, dancing and jumping at the end of a rope. As soon as she saw me she bounded over, ready to take a flying leap into my arms as if she had known me all her life. At that moment I seriously considered escaping back into the house and locking the door. As I stood there watching her, so full of the joy of living, I pictured her spending the rest of her days living in a small space at the refuge without the close human contact that she so obviously craved. Inevitably, as time passed, that wonderful spirit would be broken as she resigned herself to her fate. I grasped the rope and decided to live dangerously. That was eight years ago.

Meg is still with me, full of lightning energy and living life to the fullest. In retrospect, I am convinced that she was no more than four years old on that first day, but I am grateful for the vet whose clouded judgment enabled her to enjoy the freedom and happiness she deserved. She had been given a name at the shelter but she didn't respond to it. On the second day I experimented with several different names, hoping that she would recognize one, but I was always greeted with a blank stare.

When I was a child growing up in the farmlands of rural Yorkshire, England, farmers were inclined to give their plough horses and working dogs (not to mention a favorite cow or the occasional pig) such names as Bob, Jack, Meg or Bessie. Inspired by a sudden wave of nostalgia as I was coming to the end of my creative efforts to produce a sound that might be even vaguely recognizable to this dog, I called out "Bessie? Meg?" At the sound of "Meg" her whole demeanor changed. She became instantly alert. Her eyes brightened, her ears shot up and her head cocked to one side enquiringly. I repeated "Meg?" She attempted a long-distance high-five, and I knew my search was over. I felt an undeniable glow of success!

Meg is still a very pretty dog. Her glossy black coat is flecked with gray, gold and silver, and a black mask reaches from the top of her head to just below her eyes. A little white star shines in the middle of her forehead, and her expressive dark brown eyes are always alert and vigilant. She has the herding dog's keen intelligence and the inquisitiveness of a child, which at times can be a challenging combination. I feel sure she was once a close companion to someone, and judging by her behavior I would guess that someone to be a man. She expertly "high fives," instead of the more sedate "shake hands, and her passion for pickup trucks leads me to believe that she spent many hours in one before I knew her. In fact, this was made very obvious one day soon after she came to live with me.

I had to be out of town for a few days and a delivery man carelessly left the garden gate open. As the dog-sitter emerged through the front door to pick up the morning paper, Meg bolted past. From the window she had seen a pickup truck parked a block away on the other side of the road and, to the sitter's horror, shot down a busy street towards it, ignoring the many cars parked nearby. Meg was soon retrieved, sitting outside the cab as she waited expectantly for someone to open the door. To this day, one of her greatest joys is to perch on the front seat of my Jeep, safely fastened in a doggy seat belt, with her nose through the open window as she absorbs every sight and sound.

One of the fascinating aspects of adopting adult dogs is exploring the recesses of their minds where memories of past experiences are concealed, coloring their present lives. It is usually easy to determine which dogs have been victims of brutal treatment. Cowering, belly-crawling, rolling on their backs in abject submission, and an overpowering desire to please are all familiar signs of ill-treatment. With many of my past rescues, including one that is still with me today, I have learned to be cautious when picking up anything that could be construed as an instrument of physical punishment. A broom, a stick, or even something as innocent as a hairbrush, can cause victims of abuse to flee in terror or cringe pathetically on the ground. With other rescues, like

Meg, one gradually discovers new, interesting, and happy features of their previous lives. These unknown quantities often surface slowly; it is sometimes weeks or months before they are recognized. One such experience occurred with Meg roughly three weeks after she joined the family.

It has always been customary for me to call the name of each dog to attract his or her attention, followed by a command, such as "Max, sit!" or "Max, here!" Each dog knows his or her own name and ignores directions given to the others. After Meg had been with me long enough (or so I thought) to know my voice and recognize the different inflections, I expected her to respond accordingly. She would already sit and lie down on command and knew many other words such as "Walk," "Go upstairs," and the all-important "Go be a good dog," which galvanized her bladder into instant action. But she resolutely refused to come when I called "Meg, here!" Then one day I lost patience. I had repeatedly called her, my voice raising several octaves with frustration as she sat on her chair, calmly observing me without moving a muscle.

Finally my self-control snapped.

"Meg, COME when you are called, or you'll be in big trouble!" I threatened in a loud voice.

The response was as unexpected as it was dramatic. She sprang to her feet and like a bullet she flew to my right side, circled behind me and sat like a statue at my left heel. I felt crushed by my own stupidity. I had been using the wrong word all along, instead of taking the time to learn the commands she had already been taught. From then on "here" was dropped from her vocabulary and replaced by "Meg, come!" And come she does, with speed and alacrity, every time she is called.

Another interesting discovery was her passion for balls. She had been with me at least two months before she found an old, discarded tennis ball in some long grass. She pounced on it with such delight, before running back to drop it at my feet, that it was plain to see she had spent many happy hours with her special person, fetching, carrying, and searching for lost balls. She carried her new-found treasure all the way home, refusing to part with it for even a moment, so a different daily routine was established. Each morning and evening before meals is "ball time." A basketful of lacrosse and tennis balls is kept handy, and both Max and Meg are allowed to choose their own. Max has no interest in chasing anything, but chews ferociously on a lacrosse ball. The side benefits of this activity are pearly-white ten-year-old teeth, which have never needed cleaning. Meg, on the other hand, runs after a tennis ball again and again until she drops to the ground, exhausted. Three minutes later she is up and ready to go again. An endless supply of tennis balls has disintegrated over the years as she works off her boundless energy.

But life with Meg has not been all sweetness and light! One day she took the opportunity to herd the mailman, nipping his ankles as he fled down the garden path. (Motto: Never run from a cattle dog unless you expect to be treated like a cow.) Only a note of abject apology from me, accompanied by an expensive box of chocolates and a promise to keep Meg confined at mail-time, saved me from a daily trip to the post office a mile away to pick up my letters. Eventually, it was my son, Peter, whom she loves dearly, who broke her of this genetically determined but extremely irritating habit. Whenever he came through the door he was greeted by a sharp nip on the calf and herded into the house, until he decided enough was enough. I never asked what method he used, but it proved to be very effective. Now, instead of "herding," Meg greets him with an exuberant "high-five" from her chair, or a flurry of excitement as she races across the floor to meet him.

Although normally friendly with other dogs, Meg can be aggressive when on a leash. I learned this unexpectedly one day when a lady suddenly rounded a corner a few feet away from me on the street. Two ferocious-looking German Shepherds accompanied her. We all came to a screeching halt — all except Meg, who only a moment ago had been walking sedately by my side on a leash. As the lady hauled the Shepherds back in an effort to regroup, Meg flung herself, growling and snarling, at the two huge dogs. I wrapped her leather leash strap around my hand, jerking her back towards me, but, due to well-muscled thighs developed during "ball time," she had the strength of a maniac. By now the lady was controlling her canine escorts remarkably well, and I suffered shame and embarrassment at my own dog's antics. I wanted to shout out "Sorry. She isn't mine. I'm only walking her for a friend," but I was too engaged in a tug-of-war for polite conversation and fibs!

Finally, Meg rose up on her hind legs, straining against the leash, and with one massive jerk I managed to flip her over onto her back. With no feelings of remorse I placed a heavy foot on her stomach, anchoring her to the ground. Without waiting for my apologies the lady vanished down an adjacent alley, dragging her dogs, which were now hysterical with excitement, in a tangled knot behind her. The whole incident had taken less than five minutes, but Meg was grounded for a month. Following her outburst of socially unacceptable behavior she had to content herself with ball time and rides in the jeep.

In spite of these few lapses, Meg has generally been a model of good conduct and obedience. She sleeps on a comforter beside my bed and is the first to nuzzle me awake each morning. For the past eight years she has been an affectionate, devoted companion who would, without a doubt, lay down her life for the family she loves.

PANSY

Several months after Andy died I decided I would look for another needy dog. If this was to be one of my callings in life, the time was right. I had always felt that I could comfortably accommodate three, and now I only had Max and Meg. After weighing the pros and cons I called the local Humane Society to ask if there were "any old dogs on death row" that had been badly abused and needed a home. There was a slight pause after my blunt reference to the cages where homeless and unwanted dogs were waiting to be euthanized, then a voice answered in guarded tones.

"If you'll hold on a moment I'll put you through to someone who can help you," the voice stated primly.

In a few seconds another very pleasant voice answered and I repeated my question, but this time I rephrased it for the sake of diplomacy. "Do you have any old abused dogs that have to be put to sleep?" I asked.

"There is one," the voice answered, "But I don't think you would want her. Would you be interested in one of our others? We have plenty to choose from."

I asked if I could have a little more information about the old dog about to be "put to sleep." I was told that she had been at the shelter for five days (the requisite amount of time allowed for people to reclaim lost, stolen or strayed pets). The previous week a couple on foot had witnessed this dog being pushed out of a car. They had tried to take the number on his license plate, but the driver had accelerated and roared off, leaving the dog lying in the street.

Not knowing what else to do, these good people had brought her, dazed and confused, to the Humane Society. Additional information revealed that she was at least twelve years old, blind in one eye, and in a terribly neglected condition. In spite of her terrifying experience she didn't seem to have suffered any broken bones or internal injuries. However, she was a problem child, and the staff was finding it increasingly difficult to care for her. An infection in both eyes required twice-daily bathing, and she was on antibiotics, which had to be given by mouth. She fought and struggled, biting at everyone who tried to treat her and growling at anyone who came near.

"Quite honestly," continued the voice, sadly but firmly, "Because of her age and disposition she is totally unadoptable. She is due to be euthanized any day now."

"Perfect," I said. "I'll take her."

As I drove over to negotiate her release into my care I realized that I hadn't asked what breed she was or, if indeed, she was any known breed at all. So I began to make plans. If this turned out to be something like a Labrador, a Golden Retriever, or a German Shepherd she might have to stay in the old wolf pen until she felt comfortable with us. I hoped she wasn't akin to an aggressive Pit Bull or Doberman because I had Max and Meg to consider. They were my first priority and must be protected, but I told myself to "cross that bridge when you come to it!"

I did begin to wonder if I still had my protective mittens, left over from many years ago, and maybe a chain, if the dog had to be secured for a day or two. She might even have to be muzzled temporarily while I treated her eyes, and until she got used to us and knew she was safe. These thoughts raced through my mind until I reached the building the voice had directed me to. As they were already expecting me, I was led into a side room while someone went to get the dog.

The door opened and to my astonishment a tiny little figure, looking like a slightly pink pumpkin, waddled slowly into the room, cautiously scanning each of us with one eye. She was stripped of all her fur, and resembled a cross between a Chihuahua and a very small, naked miniature poodle. The handler explained that her coat had been so matted and dirty that they had been forced to completely shave her. It was obvious that she had lived outdoors.

After exploring the room to her satisfaction, the little dog slowly advanced towards where I was sitting in a chair against the wall. She carefully sniffed my shoes, my socks and my jeans legs, where aromas from Max and Meg still lingered, before staring up into my face with her one little bleary eye, as if to say, "Okay. I'm ready now. Let's go."

After the necessary paperwork was completed she allowed herself to be lifted onto the front seat of my Jeep and calmly settled beside me. This was no miracle, nor was it due to some instant, irresistible attraction she felt for me. It was due to something far greater than that: she seemed to know instinctively:

she was being removed from a frightening situation over which she had no control.

I named her Pansy, a flowery tribute to Rosie, my first little girl of the streets. It was soon obvious that Pansy was totally deaf; a disability I suspect was overlooked during the initial shelter examination, as it was never mentioned. I also found that she had no front teeth, so her seemingly threatening behavior had been nothing more than a harmless gesture. She couldn't hear and was barely able to see, so for this poor little discarded orphan the world must have been a dark and threatening place. Her fears were compounded at the animal shelter where complete strangers were handling her tiny body for reasons she didn't understand. Frightened and confused, she struck back in the only way she knew.

I can honestly say that from the moment I took her home Pansy never once growled at me. She never exhibited anything but affection and a longing to be loved. She submitted with good grace to the daily routine of eye baths and medications, and soon her "good" eye improved to the point where she could see almost as well as Max and Meg. Her deafness, which probably came on slowly with age, never affected her normal activities or enjoyment of life. She turned out to be strong and healthy and as her dark, thick coat grew back she transformed from an ugly duckling into a beautiful little dog. I was delighted to see how much she enjoyed her food and doggy treats, not to mention daily walks, which were always a source of excitement and exploration for her. She loved to be picked up and cuddled, and soon learned to climb the stairs to my bedroom where she would curl up beside me at night, opposite Max.

From the beginning Pansy was perfectly at ease with Meg, but it was several weeks before she and Max could work out a satisfactory relationship. He had never lived with a small dog before, and in the beginning he found it difficult to adjust to her size. He frequently trod on her, just because he didn't see her. With his huge paws and bumbling Old English sheepdog gait, Max has always had the knack of walking over anything that happens to be in his way. Even as a puppy he sometimes knocked small, unsuspecting people down in his headlong flight to some personal goal. There was really no excuse for this odd behavior as he can see perfectly well, and the hair over his eyes has always been clipped short (contrary to popular belief this does not cause blindness!). Finally we attributed his clumsiness to youthful exuberance and learned to live with it. Not so, Pansy. Each time he accidentally stumbled over her, which initially was quite often, she flew into an uncontrollable rage. Showing no fear of the one hundred and fifteen pound Goliath towering over her, she attacked the only part of his anatomy she could reach — his feet — with toothless fury until he fled the scene.

I remember one of these skirmishes very clearly. I was preparing their evening meal as they all clustered around the counter in tight formation, eyes glued to their respective bowls. Suddenly a small piece of meat flew into the air and dropped behind them. Max, in a frenzied effort to be the first to reach it, jumped backwards. In doing so he engulfed Pansy with his fuzzy behind, and without a moment's hesitation she leaped into the air, clamping her jaws tightly on his bottom. She was abruptly transported out of the kitchen, all four feet in the air, swinging from side to side as Max ran out of the door, the piece of meat still clutched in his mouth.

To his credit, Max never retaliated, and Pansy always remained victorious. Eventually they formed some kind of a truce. Max was more cautious where he trod, and Pansy learned to avoid him, frequently running under his stomach as the only avenue of escape.

It is very normal for abused and neglected dogs to form close relationships with their rescuers, and Pansy was soon closely bonded to me. I spoiled her shamelessly, trying to atone in small measure for the cruelties she had suffered at the hands of others. I hoped that at one time in her long life she had been precious to someone.

When I had to leave the house on some errand she always took up the same position on one arm of the sofa in the living room so that she could watch me through the window. When I came home she was nearly always in exactly the same spot, head slightly turned so that she could see me with her one good eye as I came up the garden path. Wriggling and rolling on the floor, she welcomed me home in grand style. When I settled down to read the morning paper, she was there at my feet, begging to be lifted up so that she could curl up on my lap for as long as I would hold her. She was far too small to jump on my bed, but I found that if I draped a blanket over the side she could climb up using her toenails and few remaining teeth to reach the top. She came down the same way, and used this form of "mountaineering" for two years until she could no longer maneuver her way either up or down and had to be lifted on and off the bed.

After about three and a half years, the sight in her good eye started to fail. Within weeks she was bumping into furniture and had to be helped down the steps when she needed to go out. By now, Pansy had been with me long enough that she was able to navigate her way through the house remarkably well, but things were getting more difficult. By then she must have been about sixteen and age was beginning to take its toll, but she never lost her happy disposition or her spunky attitude towards life.

I took her to a doggy eye specialist and discussed surgery for the cataract that had formed on her healthy eye, but after examining her he advised against it. As he pointed out, at her advanced age there were no guarantees that surgery would be successful, it was very expensive, and it would only cause her unnecessary anxiety and pain, when she had such a short time left. I knew I should make the dreaded decision to end her life, but I could not yet do what I knew was best for her.

Then one day it happened. After she had enjoyed her morning treat and an extended cuddle on my lap while I read the newspaper, I went upstairs. Pansy stayed in the living room as she normally did until I finished the necessary chores, but it was only a few minutes before I heard a slight noise and went to investigate. She was lying on the second step from the top, curled in a small, still ball, and I knew at once that she was dead. She had been trying to reach me, and her little heart had given out. She looked so peaceful, and in spite of my own intense sadness I was thankful the end had come suddenly and without trauma.

Memories of Pansy are happy ones, but even now, years later; tears come to my eyes when I think of this little dog's courage in the face of so many adversities. I remember how she was thrown away on the street, deaf and half-blind, like so much trash; I remember her will to survive, and the joyful, uncomplaining way she faced life each day. And I remember with gratitude her undying trust in me. My only sadness is that I was not able to hold her as she slipped away, but she knew I was near and she knew she was loved. I can only hope that in those last few years with us Pansy found her own little corner of heaven on earth. In my heart, I truly believe she did.

JESS

As mentioned earlier, I grew up in England, on the edge of the Yorkshire moors, surrounded by farmers and their working horses and dogs. Our home was not far from veterinarians Alf Wight and Donald Sinclair, better known as James Herriot and Siegfried Farnon of "All Creatures Great and Small" fame. We were friends long before Alf Wight wrote his beloved books, and I greatly admired the work they did. One day I told my father that I wanted to be a veterinarian, too. He was horrified and, in a voice I knew better than to argue with, laid down the law.

"No daughter of mine is going to deliver cows in a field in the middle of the night," he said, putting an end to the conversation.

In retrospect, after reading Herriot's accounts of birthing cows followed by watching the television series which portrayed the whole messy business in detail, I have to admit that my father had a valid point. Also, in pre-second-World-War England, it would have been monstrously un-ladylike.

Each summer the county fair was held on castle grounds a mile or two from where we lived. For us it was a family affair; an event looked forward to all year. My father took time off to drive my mother, my siblings and myself to the old castle, which dated back to Cromwell's time, and it was hoped that all of his patients would stay well until evening. I remember that the highlight of my young life were the sheepdog trials and the sight and smell of the huge draft horses, all gaily decked out in ribbons and bows.

For most of the day I could be found watching the trials, enthralled by the fleet Border Collies as they competed in the herding classes. It was the pre-war days of the thirties when animals enjoyed little protection from the law and were often harshly treated in an even harsher environment. A farmer's life in the "old days" was one of drudgery and hard work from predawn until after dusk, and the animal's lives were no better. When they became too old or sick to work, instead of being allowed the rest and retirement they so patently deserved, both horses and dogs were often shot by their masters. This was always distressing to me, and undoubtedly formed the basis of my rescue efforts in later years.

A farmer who competed with his dogs each year in the sheepdog trials related one of my favorite stories. He told of a young border collie that was one of the entrants in the trials where five moorland sheep were trucked in and released on a hillside above the crowd of spectators.

These sheep, raised on unfenced moorland, were elusive and often hard to manage. A different set of sheep was released for each competing dog that raced up the hill and herded them to his master, who was waiting below. Together they would guide the sheep in the shortest possible time through makeshift hurdles and into a holding pen. When this was completed, the sheep were taken away and confined elsewhere until the end of the day.

When his turn came, on command the young Border Collie streaked up the hill towards the new set of sheep that had been freed. Everyone waited expectantly below. As minutes passed with neither dog nor sheep in sight, the crowd became restless and finally derisive, hooting and hollering with good-natured banter. After the given length of time, the dog was eliminated from the competition and the show went on while the embarrassed farmer searched for his missing dog. An hour passed with no sign of the errant collie. The trials were in full swing when over the hill appeared a huge herd of moorland sheep. In the rear was the missing Border Collie, panting and weary, but still expertly herding them down to the pens. As it turned out the original little band of half-wild moorland sheep had taken flight and disappeared soon after they were released.

Not knowing which were "his" to work with, the dog had scoured the countryside, rounding up every sheep he could find. Now, satisfied that he had them all, he brought them to his master waiting below. There was a happy reunion as the dog jumped into his master's arms, then he was carried off the field as the crowd clapped and cheered. Other canine contestants were later given the task of returning the flock to their moorland home.

The Second World War came and went. England changed, and life as I had known it changed forever. After I came to the United States, and later began my mission of rescuing old abused dogs, I often remembered with affection the hard-working sheepdogs in my native country. Each time I returned to England on vacation I tried to find at least one that had toiled all its life for little reward and bring it back with me to America. I searched diligently in the farming community, contacting old farmers I had known many years before; I phoned British rescue groups, and at one point advertised. The only offers I received were not what I had in mind: puppies, young dogs in training, and dogs that had never worked but were available for money. I finally gave up.

It is strange how things you wish for and strive for sometimes happen in the most unexpected way. It might be achievement of a goal that had seemed beyond your grasp, or an elusive, unfulfilled dream. Then, when you are about to accept the inevitability of failure, a different — and sometimes even better — solution presents itself.

After Pansy died, my quest for old, abused dogs again came to a grinding halt. Meg was at least eleven years old and Max was approaching ten, elderly for his breed and enormous size. We were about to remain a household of three when out of the blue a call came from one of the local animal shelters. The supervisor knew that over the years I had taken many aging dogs, victims of brutal treatment. She also knew I was a psychotherapist, consequently committed to healing a broken spirit as well as a broken body.

"We have a case of extreme cruelty," she said, after the initial pleasantries. "We have just taken in more than twenty dogs from a puppy mill and they are all in a deplorable condition. I have one I think you might like to work with. She's approximately eight years old and must have been very badly abused because she is terrified of everyone and everything. It is hard to place traumatized older dogs, and we feel she is not eligible for adoption. If you can't take her she is to be euthanized."

"What breed is she?" I asked, now curious even though I knew that would be the least of my concerns. Her next words were the culmination of my half-forgotten dream.

"A Border Collie." she replied.

The next day Peter and I went to collect Jess and bring her to her "forever home." A wispy little creature in a crouching position with body close to the floor crept into the office at the heels of the supervisor. When she was led across the room to where we were sitting, she immediately rolled onto her back in humble submission. As I gently stroked her, she sat up and put her head on my knee, her whole body shaking. Terrified and confused, she was ready to follow anyone who had a kind word for her, and it was easy to recognize her sweet, gentle disposition in spite of her overwhelming terror. She had been given an early morning bath at the shelter, but the pungent odor of urine and feces still clung to her body, a reminder of the filth she had been forced to live in, perhaps for years.

As soon as the necessary papers were completed Peter lifted Jess into the car and we headed for home.

She exhibited many signs of deprivation, the first being within minutes of arriving at the house. I let her off the leash as soon as we closed the front door and she obediently followed us into the living room. A few moments later I watched her creeping across the floor to a small piece of cardboard that was lying on the carpet. Looking back at us fearfully, in case she recognized signs of anger, she timidly picked up the strip of cardboard and bolted it down. This, together with her bony frame, clearly indicated neglect to the point of starvation. I wondered how long it had been since she and all the other victims had seen food before this brutal, money-grubbing operation had been uncovered.

Another sign of deprivation was her anxiety concerning water. She would lie beside a water bowl — one of many scattered about our house and garden — guarding it, as though afraid it would disappear. At intervals she would get up to take a few laps from the bowl before returning to her former position, lying protectively beside it. This went on for several days, and although she never interfered with Max or Meg when they came to drink from the same bowl, her need to stay close to water seemed to imply more than thirst. I could only think that fresh water was a luxury that the puppy mill victims seldom enjoyed. After a week or two, the compulsions to stay near water and to search for scraps of inedible trash waned, and eventually disappeared altogether. Jess had begun the long road to recovery.

At that time I knew very little about puppy mills. I understood that such things existed but was totally unaware of the callousness and cruelty typically found in this type of operation. To the uninformed the term "puppy mill" could conjure up visions of happy little puppies frolicking with their mothers in the country. Unfortunately, although the offspring were often sick and dying, especially when transported cross-country en masse to pet stores, the true, heartbreaking stories lay with the mothers—the breeding females. Typically, these poor wretched creatures lived out their lives in cages, in some cases never even seeing the light of day. Many of them lived on wire, stacked like unhappy chickens raised for slaughter. They never knew the joy of running free over cool grass or feeling the summer breeze on their faces. They were prisoners for life, destroyed when no longer useful, and I was sickened to learn that, in many of these businesses, execution was carried out by drowning or a bullet in the head.

The sole function in life for these victims was to produce as many litters as their bodies could stand, which might mean years of misery. In Jess's case the cages were small and her calloused, heavily scabbed feet attested to the fact that the adult females were forced to permanently sit or lie on wire, making the occasional removal of waste from the cages an easier chore for the puppy mill owners. When someone eventually came across the horrifying scene and called the police, no food or water was found. Sad to say, although apprehended and taken to court, the perpetrators escaped and were never seen again.

Of course there may be so-called "puppy mills" that are not deserving of this title— places where puppies and their mothers are provided with comfortable housing, daily exercise and nutritious food; where the females are not expected to produce litters every six months like automatons and are retired in a humane and timely manner. These are not what this story is about.

Four of Jess's teeth — the canines — had been broken in half. Possibly this was no accident as the toe nails on all four feet had been cruelly mutilated, cut far back into the paws in a procedure that must have caused extreme pain. One can only assume that these barbaric practices were carried out to prevent the prisoners from biting and scratching the cages in a futile attempt to escape, and possibly to enable them to balance on the bottom of the cage without getting caught in the wire. Injuries might mean loss of a breeding female and consequently loss of income. Jess was still limping when we adopted her, and under her sparse black and white coat, her ribs and hip bones stuck out. She had very few eyelashes and, oddly enough, no "eyebrows." The skin above her eyes was bare. It seemed as though the starved body had shed every particle of hair and flesh that was not essential for survival.

Initially I fed her four small meals a day, and although she ate ravenously she had difficulty keeping even small amounts of food down. As her shrunken stomach expanded she was able to tolerate more, and after several weeks there was a noticeable weight gain. Another six months and she had gained all of the weight recommended by the family vet. He warned me, however, that there could still be adverse consequences to internal organs from her prolonged starvation.

She did, in fact, suffer one grand mal seizure soon after she came to us, but happily since then she has continued to grow physically strong and healthy. As her weight increased her eyelashes and eyebrows grew back, her coat became thick and shiny, and her body lost its frail, waiflike appearance.

But even as the broken body mended, it seemed as though the crushed spirit would never heal. Anyone holding a stick, broom, or any club-like object caused Jess to cringe in fear. If I came across her unexpectedly, she would sink to the floor, head pressed against the ground, and if I reached out to gently caress her she would cower and roll onto her back. If I verbally corrected Max, who is not deaf but has a permanent case of selective hearing, I would find Jess a quivering mass under the sofa. (I always had to stop to comfort and reassure her, so Max often escaped scot-free after some infraction of the rules!) Before eating, Jess would look for permission, even when the food was set in front of her. When the other dogs scrambled into the house from outside, it was Jess who waited on the doorstep, not daring to come in until she knew she would not be punished. She was so humbly obedient I felt almost embarrassed to tell her to do anything, and really there was little need because she was my slave, constantly searching my face trying to anticipate my wishes.

After the first day, I noticed her tail wagged almost constantly, and three days after we picked her up from the shelter as I sat writing at the table I heard a steady thumping sound. Looking down I saw Jess fast asleep at my feet, closed eyes twitching as her tail beat out a rhythmic tattoo on the carpet. She was clearly in the middle of a beautiful dream, and I hoped with all my heart that her new family played at least a small part in her happy fantasy.

From the beginning, it was obvious that at some time in her life she had been a working dog. As no sheep or cattle were available, she concentrated on Max and Meg. Sometimes Meg was herded through the open gate into the old wolf pen, with Jess then positioning herself across the opening to prevent an escape. Sometimes a surprised Max was guided over to me, with Jess running back and forth at his heels to urge him on or giving an occasional push with her nose, but she never applied the traditional sheepdog nip of authority. Before too long all three began to bond, and herding was abandoned in favor of play.

Within three or four months a tight relationship developed between Jess and Meg, and they now run a mile or two together each day.

It always delights me to watch Jess in motion, stretching out like a thoroughbred racehorse as she gallops across the fields for the pure joy of running.

Jess adores Peter. She recognizes his footsteps as he turns the corner at the end of the block from his own home, and is eagerly waiting as he reaches our front door. With tail wagging furiously she peers through the mail slot on the porch wall, ready to greet him in a transport of delight. Plainly, she has never forgotten that he was the first to lift her into the car and drive her to safety. But for many months she was suspicious and fearful of all other men. After a few weeks she learned to tolerate Susie's husband when he reached out to her, but retreated to a bedroom hideaway when any other male entered the house. Sometimes her anxious face could be seen peering over the upstairs banister, but she never ventured down until the visitor left. Even female friends were inspected from a safe distance.

Outside, if she met a man coming towards her, Jess would lie flat on the ground until he passed. If he happened to be wearing a cowboy hat and boots she panicked. This piqued my curiosity and supported my belief that she had lived and worked on a farm or ranch in her younger days. Perhaps she had been harshly trained and punished for mistakes that she didn't understand. This would explain her fears, her absolute obedience and her compulsion to please.

I started to explore words and whistles that might sound familiar to her. The word "watch," which I used inadvertently one day, caused an instant reaction — ears forward, body rigid, eyes searching. "Wait" caused her to stand like a statue, ready for immediate action while listening intently for the next command. A whistle brought her racing to my side, alert to my directions, and on the command "down" she dropped like a stone, chin on paws. Clearly, she had received thorough training, probably long before she became a puppy mill victim.

I searched for anyone who had sheep in this corner of cattle country. Eventually we located a farmer who lived many miles from town. He trained sheepdogs that he entered in trials, and he agreed to try Jess out on his small flock of sheep. However when he heard that she had been a breeding female, confined to a cage in a puppy mill, he was skeptical.

"Don't expect much," he told me. "She will probably follow the sheep, because that's her natural instinct. But to be a herding dog she would have to be trained."

To demonstrate, he brought out two of his Australian shepherds. Faultlessly they worked the sheep, first singly and then together. It was a delight to watch them.

Then it was Jess's turn. Completely absorbed by the sheep, she showed no fear of the farmer. At first he attached a long cord to her collar, but as soon as he realized that she stayed close beside him he released her from the cord and directed her towards the sheep with whistles and commands. The sheep were standing at the far end of the field. Jess knew exactly what was expected of her, and circling the small flock she expertly guided them to the waiting farmer.

Responding to verbal commands, whistles, and hand signals, she effortlessly guided the sheep in any direction he indicated. At the end of the demonstration she penned the flock with little assistance from the shepherd. He stared at her in admiration.

"This dog must have been raised on a farm," he said. "She knows sheep and she's been thoroughly trained. You've got yourself a top working dog, lady."

Considering the fact that a total stranger was directing her and she was responding to an unfamiliar voice, I was immensely proud of the way Jess carried out her assigned task. In addition, it was rewarding to know that we could now add one more missing piece to the puzzle of Jess's mysterious past.

Why fate had dealt with her so cruelly is something we will never know. The only certainty is that someone cared so little about this loving, faithful dog that they abandoned her to a life of misery and suffering, to be caged for life in a puppy mill. But she is safe now. As for me, I have fulfilled my goal and achieved my half-forgotten dream: a working Border Collie that had suffered years of abuse has found her "forever home" with me.

Now, two years later, Jess is moving on. Like our beautiful Brandy of so long ago, she is gradually overcoming her terrors. In the house she never leaves me, following at my heels from room to room. She no longer crawls and cringes, and her tail still wags constantly. When I stretch out my hand to caress her she comes gladly and without fear. She sits beside me when I am working, and sleeps nestled against me at night. She will always be timid with strangers, but she now greets them shyly when she realizes they mean no harm. To her great delight, she and I return to the farm and the shepherd several times a year so that she can satisfy her natural instincts and retain her sheepherding skills.

The family loves to spoil Jess, and she receives the attention graciously, giving all her doggy love in return. Meg is her idol, Max is her guardian, and Jess, the puppy mill survivor, has found her heaven on earth at last.

A blue van is turning into the driveway, drawing my thoughts back into the present. A man gets out and opens the double doors at the back. As I go outside to greet them I can hear him talking softly: "It's okay, girl. You're home now. Come on, sweetheart."

He tugs gently at the leash and I see a white head appear. The dog jumps slowly out of the van and stands motionless on the ground, completely indifferent to her surroundings. She shows no reaction — no fear, no excitement, no curiosity. Her head is lowered, almost to the ground, and it swings rhythmically from side to side. Her eyes are a striking blue, completely devoid of any emotion. The hopeless stance and blank stare cause a wave of sadness to engulf me. I reach out to stroke her and there is no response. She continues to stand motionless with only the head swinging from side to side.

I take her leash and the three of us start toward the house, I to complete the adoption papers assuring good care and a permanent home for the rest of her life. The dog follows automatically, head hanging low. She walks slowly and stiffly, her legs weak from years of confinement.

"There must be a dog somewhere in that shell of a body," the man accompanying us says. "How can anyone do that to a defenseless animal?"

"Does she have a name?" I ask.

"No, she only had a number. But we named her Daisy," he replied.

I look down at the silent figure trailing along behind us and make a solemn promise to myself: It may take six months, it may take a year, but one day I will crack that shell and at last the spirit that has been imprisoned for so long will be free.

EPILOGUE

It happened one cold winter's night some time last year and I am only now feeling the urge to share this remarkable experience. At the time I was sitting cozily ensconced in an armchair, the lights low and an after-dinner drink in my hand. I was feeling pleasantly sleepy and relaxed. In the fireplace a log fire burned, and the cold night air outside was still. The curtains were open and I could see stars dotting the sky and a silvery moon peeking over the trees in the far distance. My two dogs — Daisy, an Old English sheepdog, and Jess, a Border Collie — were dozing peacefully by my side.

As I half-lay in the easy chair, my mind lazily drifting, I began to feel a "presence." I became aware of a slight tingling sensation and a strange aura that I had never felt before. I leaned forward and looked down at my sleeping dogs. I saw Jess stir. Suddenly she sat up and cocked her head as her ears flew into listening position. Her tail thumped gently on the floor and it was then that I realized her eyes were tracking something that I could not see. Within seconds Daisy, too, was awake, her eyes concentrated on something in the middle of the living room floor. Then without a sound both dogs rose and silently crept away.

In the darkness of the room I began to make out shadowy figures. I blinked my eyes several times but the figures remained, sitting quietly in a circle. I could count at least a dozen of them and they all seemed to be perfectly at ease, both with each other and with me. A great sense of peace and tranquility suffused my whole body, and I was aware of a happiness that I had not felt for many months. In the stillness of the room I heard a small sound, almost like a sigh, followed by a gentle touch on my bare arm and the familiar feel of something soft pressing against my leg.

Many years ago when I was a small child, my Irish grandmother told me tales of Ireland. Her stories of fairies and goblins and the "little people" fascinated me so much I could almost see the villages and people she was describing. She told me of a mystical veil between this world and the next, and of a "thin place" described in Celtic folklore where the "other world" is just beyond the veil.

Could this be the "thin place" that my grandmother spoke of with such awe and respect? But who were the shadowy figures, and what was this wonderful feeling of peace and love that I felt? There was a slight shuffling in the circle and I could now see the outline of many dogs — two very small, six or seven very large, and the rest of varying shapes and sizes .Was this my imagination or had I unwittingly entered the spirit world of animals? Or had they chosen to enter mine? Before I could try to make any sense of what was happening, I felt rather than heard a deep voice:

"Now that we are all here," it rumbled, "we can begin. I am Jock, and I am the oldest so I will take it upon myself to lead this group." His manner of speech was of the early nineteen hundreds, cultured but with just a hint of Yorkshire accent.

"For those of you who don't understand the proceedings, and why we are here, I will explain. This is the night that we have waited for," he continued, "when for a brief period of time we are able to connect with those we have loved on Earth. But this is only possible with those who have truly loved us and who believe we will meet again when they, too, pass over. Tonight was the night designated by our (his voice dropped reverently) Higher Power and we are now in what some humans call the "thin place." The veil is lifted and for a short time, we will be reunited with the one who gave us the security and happiness that all dogs long for. Everyone here loved Missy. She gave us a piece of heaven in a world of cruelty and suffering, and we want her to know that we will be waiting for her when it comes time for her to leave that place they call Earth. Mind you," he added hastily, "I have no cause to complain. Compared with the rest of you I had a good life down there."

"So what are we doing here, Jock?" asked another member of the circle.

"We are all going to tell our stories of life on Earth before Missy found us and took us to our "forever home." She always longed to know the mystery of our past lives, and tonight those mysteries will be revealed to her. Also, our presence here will help her to form a bond with us for the next world — the one we have all come from tonight."

Missy? I couldn't believe my ears. The shadowy figures were talking about me, but how was I able to see and hear them? I leaned back in my chair, prepared to enjoy the fantasy unfolding in my living room, but I could not shake the feeling that I had stepped into another world where space and time did not exist. Was it just a dream, inspired by the warm, sleepy atmosphere and a glass of good wine? I will never know. But the tales my grandmother told me were starting to take shape. I could almost feel the mystical veil that shrouded the "thin place" of Celtic lore parting, and tonight I was among the abused animals that I had loved and nurtured over the years. I felt at one with them, and listening closely, I found myself able to interpret the language they used amongst themselves.

Jock spoke again. "We all have our special stories of life on Earth. Tonight we have been brought together to share them, although I know some are painful to remember." Jock's voice was tinged with sadness as he said this, but brightened as he continued, "And I will begin by telling you mine."

"I was born many, many years ago in a land called England. On Earth I had the body and soul of a Scottish Deerhound, and nearly all my ancestors had lived in Scotland. Most of them belonged to very rich people and their job was to hunt and chase deer so their masters could shoot them. I'm glad I didn't have to do that."

"If you were a Scottish Deerhound, what were you doing in England?" a small voice piped up.

There was a slight pause before Jock began again. "I will tell you why I was in England," he replied patiently, "but you will have to listen carefully because mine is quite a long story. It all began in 1927, which is the year I was born.

"My father was a very handsome dog. His master entered him in many big shows and he won many prizes. My mother lived in England and was sent to Scotland to meet my father. She came back and after a while she had six puppies, including me. I had three brothers and two sisters, and we all had a very happy time together. Then, when we were about two months old, people started to come and look at us, and one by one my brothers and sisters disappeared. My master said he was very happy because they all went to "nice people." I didn't really know what he meant until Mr. Robert came and took me home with him.

"Mr. Robert was a very fine gentleman who lived in England. He had a big house with several employees, and everyone was very kind to me. They fed me well and played with me, and when I was older Tom, the handyman, took me for walks in the country every day. There were a lot of sheep on the moorlands close to our home and I would see them on our walks. When we got close to them they always ran away in a big bunch, and then they would turn around and stare at us and waggle their tails. They made funny bleating noises and didn't smell good. I found them very exciting.

"Then I started to do something bad. When I was about a year old I began to sneak out of the house and jump the garden fence. I wanted to see the sheep so badly that when I found them I chased them all over the fields. It was fun for me, but one day the farmer saw me and came to my master's house. He was very angry and told my master what I had been doing. It was lambing time, he said, and he would lose the lambs as well as the sheep. Mr. Robert told him that he was very sorry, he would pay for any damage, and he would see that it didn't happen again. But it did."

"So what happened then?" asked another voice anxiously.

"Every chance I got I went back to those silly sheep and chased them, sometimes nipping their heels to make them run faster. When the farmer came again to the house I knew I was in trouble. Later that day I heard Mr. Robert talking to Tom. 'Tom,' he said in a very serious tone of voice. 'I'm afraid Jock is going to have to be put down. Once a dog starts chasing sheep it is hard to break him of the habit, and I don't think it is fair to Jock to keep him chained up. And if I sell him I don't know what kind of a home he might get. I think it would be kinder to shoot him and be done with it.'

"In the old days that's what they did. Shoot us. No going to the vet to be "put to sleep."

Jock paused a moment to let his words sink in. There were appropriate sounds of horror and disbelief coming from some members of the circle.

"Of course at that time I didn't understand what he was telling Tom," Jock continued, "I only knew that I was in big trouble. Then I heard him say to Tom, 'We'll put him down tomorrow,' and to keep me chained up in an old kennel in the backyard. I ate my supper outside and felt very lonely."

"Did he beat you?" asked a soft, tremulous voice. "I'm Brandy. I was a Borzoi, a Russian Wolfhound, and I was beaten a lot. Most of the time I didn't understand why."

"No. He didn't ever beat me," replied Jock thoughtfully. "He was always kind to me, and I think he was really fond of me in his own way. He thought he was doing what was best for me. But all that night I stayed outside in the dog house, wondering what was going to happen to me. I had never been chained up before. I had always slept at the foot of Mr. Robert's bed, so this was very confusing for me. I howled a few times but no one came.

"It was very early the next morning when I heard someone at the front door. I was still chained to the dog house, but I could watch through the fence and I saw a young girl, about ten years old, standing on the steps, waiting. After a few moments, Charles, the butler opened the door and in a stern voice asked the child what she wanted."

Jock hesitated for a few moments.

In the silence of the room the years melted away. I was again that small child, standing on the doorstep of a strange house, shaking with fear but determined to carry out my mission. I had dressed hastily in an assortment of strange clothes and I was in such a state of anxiety I had not even stopped to wash or brush my hair. My voice trembled slightly as I addressed the austere looking butler standing in the doorway.

"I hear you are going to kill your dog. I have come to take him," I began in a shaky voice, "if you will let me have him."

"I will have to speak to Mr. Robert," the butler said over his shoulder as he disappeared back into the house. Soon "Mr. Robert" was at the door.

"What is it you want, child, and who are you?"

When faced with the master of the household my courage began to evaporate, but I managed to stammer out the reason for my sudden appearance on his doorstep. After listening patiently for a few minutes, Mr. Robert invited me into his study to hear the rest of the story. My passionate plea for mercy was effective and I experienced my first rescue in the form of a huge, sheep-chasing deerhound!

Out of the shadows of my living room Jock began to speak again. "I couldn't hear anything else so I went back to lie in the dog house, and the next thing I knew Tom was coming out of the back door and fastening a leash to my collar. Tom worked in the stable with the horses most of the time and he was always nice to me, so I became very excited. I thought he had come to take me for a walk, but instead he led me into Mr. Robert's study. The little girl was perched in a huge armchair looking very nervous, and my master was sitting at his desk, talking to her in a kind, fatherly manner. After a while he told her she could take me home with her, and that is what she did."

"How did Missy know you were going to be, er, shot?" asked Brandy, the Russian Wolfhound, in a small, worried voice.

"It was something to do with tea parties, and Missy's mother, and Tom dating a friend's housemaid." Jock sounded a little impatient. "Oh well, what does it matter? The main thing is that Missy heard about it and, thank goodness, she got there just in time."

"I never knew the whole conversation that took place between Mr. Robert and Missy, but she was so happy and excited I knew everything was going to be all right. On the walk home she kept stopping to hug me and tell me she loved me already."

"I was very happy in my new home. There were many other animals there, some of them wild creatures that had been injured. Missy's father was a country doctor and he often treated small animals that she and her brother brought home: little rabbits that were found in cruel leg traps, and squirrels or other animals that had been hurt on the road.

"In my new home there was a cat called John, and two sheepdogs who were very friendly. Their names were Max and Judy, and we had a good time playing together on the lawn. There were high fences all around the garden so there was no danger of any of the dogs getting out, especially me. And in a paddock at the back of the house there was a horse, and a donkey called Molly. I liked to go and talk to them through the fence, but I never tried to chase them.

"I loved to smell the cages where injured animals were kept, and to go with Missy when she fed them and tended to their wounds. When they were well enough to be set free Missy and her brother took them out into the fields with all of us dogs, and we would watch them run away. They were glad to be going home.

"Almost right away Missy started my training. Some of the farmers were patients of Missy's father and. they let us walk in their fields amongst the flocks of sheep and herds of milk cows. They even helped with my training, shouting out advice and words of encouragement.

"Missy was very strict with me, and after a few weeks I learned to walk by her side and ignore the sheep. I always got treats when I behaved well — pieces of meat that tasted so good I didn't even want to chase the sheep. It wasn't fun anymore. Those days were heaven on earth, but on Earth nothing lasts forever.

"It was 1939 when everything started to change. People went about with long faces and sometimes they huddled together in groups, talking in serious voices. The men, and some of the women, wore funny clothes in the streets, which they called "uniforms," and carried strange packs that hung from their shoulders down to their waist. They called these "gas masks," and when they practiced wearing them they looked strange and frightening. At the end of our house was a stone building and Missy worked with sticky tape, sealing up all the windows and stuffing blankets around the bottom of the door. She told her parents that this was for Max and Judy and me, and John, 'just in case the Nazis gas us.' I didn't know what it meant, but it didn't sound good.

"The horse and the donkey were sold to farmers, as there was no food for them at our house. We had no heat and the winter was cold, so I was glad that I had a good thick coat. We dogs had no more meat or treats, but were no worse off than the humans.

"Missy's brother was the first to go. He had on a uniform and a gas mask on his shoulder. By that time he was a doctor too, and went to fight a German called

Rommel in the desert far away. Then my beloved Missy came to me one day and kneeled down beside me. There were tears in her eyes as she hugged me and told me to be a good boy and look after things at home.

"I'll see you again soon," she said. "Look after Mum and Dad." And she walked out of the door, wearing the same sort of uniform clothes as her brother and the same gas mask on her shoulder.

"By this time Max and Judy, and even John, had grown old and left for the Other World, so I was the only one at home with Missy's parents. They tried to take good care of me but it wasn't the same. No more walks. No more treats No more little wild creatures.

"I was about thirteen years old and becoming slow and stiff when something terrifying happened. I was in the garden with Missy's mother and father when we heard a loud droning sound overhead. We all looked up to see what this strange noise was, so loud and frightening. The sky was filled with huge objects, all moving towards us. Soon there were whistling noises above and things were raining down from the sky. When the whistling stopped huge flames shot out of the ground and the earth shook so violently we almost fell down. I tried to reach the old people so that I could take care of them, like Missy told me to, but before I could get to them there was another whistling sound overhead. I heard my name being called as the old people tried to run into the house. That is the last thing I remember on Earth.

"The next thing I knew I was standing in the most beautiful place I had ever seen. There was no sun, but all was warmth and light. Shade trees dotted the landscape and all manner of animals were lying comfortably in the long grass underneath leafy branches. There was a soft glow everywhere, and the colors in this heavenly place were indescribably radiant and lovely. I saw sheep and cows, horses and pigs from the slaughterhouses on Earth, standing peacefully in the long green grass. There were battery chickens, freed from the horrors of their earthly life. They were unafraid and blending with foxes and all manner of other wild animals that touched noses with each other and licked each other's faces. Everything seemed to be filled with love and happiness.

"John was there, and Max and Judy, lying in the soft grass. They ran to greet me, looking young again as they welcomed me to this wonderful land. Other dogs were playing in the meadows, chasing balls and Frisbees that magically flew through the air, and some swam in a sparkling blue lake. I felt like a puppy again, not old and stiff any more. I cannot begin to express my feelings of utter joy at being in this heavenly place."

There was silence among the group clustered around my living room floor. Then Jock spoke again.

"Tonight our time here on Earth is short, but you will all have a chance to speak and to touch Missy before the veil closes and we return to our own land. Rosie, you were Missy's first rescue in this place they call America. I know you have a sad story to tell, but so have all the others. Tell us about your life before Missy."

One by one my heavenly dogs told their stories of life on Earth before rescue, revealing the mysteries that had plagued me with each victim. They told of their suffering, the cruelties and abandonment, until I felt the tears streaming down my cheeks. The last tale was told and the room fell silent. Then, one by one, I felt a soft nose touching my face. I tried to reach out and hug every one of them but my arms were filled with emptiness. The mysterious veil closed and I was alone in a lonely room.

Had I really experienced the "thin place" that my grandmother so fondly described? Or was it all a beautiful dream — sleep brought on by the warmth of the fire, a glass of good wine, and the quiet solitude of the night? I only know that for a brief time I experienced an outpouring of love such as I had never known before and will only know again when the veil is lifted and I pass into that heavenly place of eternal peace and love.

ABOUT THE AUTHOR

Monica Agnew-Kinnaman was born in England and came to America after serving in a British anti-aircraft artillery regiment during World War II. Although she had dogs all her life, since her husband died the last fifteen years have been devoted to taking old, abused and abandoned dogs that nobody wanted, so they can end their days in peace and comfort, and with lots of love. She has a doctorate in Psychology but is now retired. She lives in Colorado with Jess, an eleven year old Border Collie, and Lilly, an almost-fourteen-year old Old English Sheepdog. She also has a son and daughter who live in Colorado.

If you've enjoyed this book, please find Monica's children's fiction series about Samson, a loveable English Sheepdog who wants to be a hero like the knights of old. Available at Amazon in Kindle eBook, black and white print, and full color print.

Made in the USA
Monee, IL
10 December 2023

48715973R00079